IDENTIFICATION
&
POLICE LINE-UPS

by
WILLIAM E. RINGEL
Judge, Criminal Court of the
City of New York

GOULD PUBLICATIONS
208-01 Jamaica Avenue
Jamaica, N.Y., 11428

To my dear

IRMA

with whom I have always

"Identified"

FOREWORD

Judge William E. Ringel has been identified with the administration of the criminal law for almost thirty years. At present he is the Senior Judge of the Criminal Court of the City of New York. His experience, scholarly attainments and fine analytical mind were reflected in his prior works dealing with the constitutional guarantees against unlawful arrests, searches, seizures and confessions.

In this volume on Criminal Identification and Police Lineups, Judge Ringel has again demonstrated his exceptional ability to collate and analyze what appear to be conflicting opinions so as to make crystal clear the principles of law involved and how they are to be applied. The book has been well planned. It contains a full and carefully detailed index which provides a ready reference to almost any portion of the many topics considered. The cases selected for discussion are not limited to the leading cases but include many others that are relevant or pertinent to the question being considered. The manner in which the subject is treated not only brings the reader abreast of the rapidly changing Criminal Law but illuminates the way for the future. The book is an exhaustive study of a most important phase of the Criminal Law, expertly done.

The bench and bar of the Criminal Courts are indeed indebted to Judge Ringel for this valuable contribution to the field of Criminal Law.

Vincent A. Massi
Assistant Administrative Judge
Criminal Court of the City of New York

TABLE OF CONTENTS

TABLE OF CONTENTS (continued)

TABLE OF CONTENTS (continued)

INTRODUCTION

The psychological and legal problems implicit in the area of identification in criminal proceedings have recently been highlighted by the United States Supreme Court in three landmark decisions, <u>United States v. Wade</u> (388US218); <u>Gilbert v. California</u> (388US263); and <u>Stovall v. Denno, Warden</u> (388US293).

These cases deal with police lineup identification and the application of the Fifth, Sixth and Fourteenth Amendments of the United States Constitution thereto.

The book is divided roughly into two parts. The first part deals with the methods and techniques of criminal identification in general. It encompasses the psychological factors involved in identification by sight as well as the scientific and non-scientific methods employed in the field of identification. Areas for cross-examination are indicated in some detail.

The second part of the book contains an analysis of the three opinions in <u>Wade</u>, <u>Gilbert</u> and <u>Stovall</u> and lineup identification. The opinions themselves are also set forth in full.

I wish to express my appreciation to Lt. John Sullivan of the Legal Bureau of the New York City Police Department for his helpful suggestions.

March 15, 1968   W.E.R.

PART I
IDENTIFICATION

A. <u>HISTORICAL BACKGROUND</u>.

Throughout history, man's ability to survive depended largely on his ability to discern and to identify those things which were inimicable to his safety and existence, and those which were not. To feed himself and his family he had to be able to distinguish between edible and poisonous plants (the palatable mushroom and the poisonous toadstool), as well as the edible insects and animals, and those which were best avoided. He had to learn which animals he could domesticate and which were best left alone.

In his relations with his fellow-man, the same rule applied. Which were his friends and which were his enemies? In a tooth-and-claw society, all strangers were enemies, to be killed on sight. On the other hand, prompt recognition of a friend, e.g. a member of one's own tribe, meant the difference between life and death.

Thus, the ability to recognize, to identify and to be identified was of paramount importance in a primitive society. To achieve this most necessary and desirable aim, primitive tribes mar and scar their bodies. The scars stand out like ridges. Tatoo marks are also used - bright and light colors are employed. Some tribes remove their 2 front teeth or file them into odd shapes. Some, like the Ubangi, distend their lower lips so that they approach the size of saucers. Others, like the pygmy Bakwa, have long upper lips, depressed noses with enormous alae, while the Watusi are blessed by nature with great height - 7 feet tall. There is no mistaking them.

The mark of Cain, described in Genesis, was not a mark of disgrace, but the mark of the tribe which agreed to accept him after he had been banished. It was granted to Cain as a mark of clemency so that he might not be mistaken for an enemy and thus slain on sight.

Such a system, disfigurement for identification, is simple indeed. It might solve many problems involving inheritance, pretenders to thrones, and the like. However, it is scarcely acceptable in our civilization. (Wilder and Wentworth, "Personal Identification"; Vergat, "LES RITES DES PRIMITES DE L'OUGANQUI," Paris 1936).

We use more sophisticated methods. The armed forces use uniforms, pass words, serial numbers, flags and banners, "dog tags," Identification (I.D.) cards, and even name plates on uniforms in addition to regimental and division insignia and insignia of rank. Thus we try to distinguish friend from foe. In civilian life we have social security numbers, passports, automobile operator's licenses, credit cards, etc. etc. All of these items are of help and through them identity can be established, with more or less accuracy.

B. PROBLEMS OF IDENTIFICATION IN CRIMINAL PROCEEDINGS.

However, identifying the culprit as the perpetrator of a criminal act is another matter. Many factors come into play. For one thing, the luxury of time, required to identify the culprit, is absent; nor does the criminal

4

leave his social security number behind.

Crimes are often committed in a flash. Who did it? In many criminal prosecutions, identification of the culprit has proven to be a most difficult and most distressing problem. As a result, many innocent men have been convicted. See e.g. In re Campbell (Court of General Sessions, Oct 25, 1945, NYLJ, Oct. 26, 1945), More than one innocent man has been hung because of erroneous identification. And often enough, the error was made, not by vindictive people, by by well-meaning, honest citizens whose only motive was to relate the truth as they thought they saw it. It would be pointless to list the many cases in which this has occurred.

It is a basic tenet of our criminal law that no person shall be convicted of a crime unless each and every element of the crime has been proved beyond a reasonable doubt (People v. Schryver, 42NY17). Identification of the defendant as the perpetrator is one of those elements. His identity must also be established beyond a reasonable doubt. (People v. Noland, 27AD(2)663; cf. People v. Hunter, 20NY(2)789; People v. Caserta, 19NY(2)18).

The difficulties in the area of identification have long been recognized by the courts. "One of the most stubborn problems in the administration of the criminal law is to establish identity by the testimony of witnesses to whom an accused was previously unknown, from quick observation under stress or when, as here, there was no particular reason to note the person's identity." (People v. Caserta, 19NY(2)18,21).

C. WHAT IS IDENTIFICATION.

In a criminal prosecution identification is proof of identity. It is the establishing, beyond a reasonable doubt "that a person. . . before the court is the very same that he is alleged . . . or charged to be; as where a witness recognizes the prisoner at the bar as the same person whom he saw committing the crime; . . ." (Blacks Law Dictionary, 4th Edition); "recognition of a person as having been seen previously"(Dictionary of Legal Terms by Irving Shapiro).

D. IDENTITY.

Identity, in the Law of Evidence means "sameness; the fact that a . . . person . . . before the court is the same . . . as charged to be." (Blacks, ibid.)(emphasis added)

E. IDENTIFICATION - OPINION EVIDENCE.

Identification is almost always a matter of opinion concerning a fact (Medsker v. State, 70NE(2)182, 183, 224Ind587; Germinder v. Machinery Mutual Ins. Assn., 94NY1108, 1109, 120Iowa614).

"The opinions of ordinary witnesses -- those not experts -- may be received as to:

1. Matters of color, weight, size, light and darkness, and inference of identity as to race, language, persons, visibility, sounds, and the like (Laubach v. Cooley, 283Pa366, 129Atl.88,89. See note, 70ALR532, 540; Commonwealth v. Sturtivant, 117Mass122, 19 Am.Rep.401; Townsend v. Brundage, 4Hun264; Miller v. City of New York, 104AppDiv33, 93NYS227).

2. The state of emotion exhibited by a person, e.g., whether he appeared to be angry or jesting. (<u>Blake v. People,</u> 73NY586, annotated L.R.A. 1918A721.)

3. The apparent physical condition of a person, which is open to ordinary observation. For example, a lay witness may testify as to a person's general strength, vigor, feebleness, illness, and his comparative condition from day to day . . . .

F. <u>IDENTITY AND LIKENESS.</u>

The witness may be asked whether he knows a certain person, and if so, whether he is the person indicated. See authorities reviewed in note, L.R.A. 1918A713. The <u>admissibility</u> of the testimony is not affected by the fact that the <u>witness is unable to testify</u> positively, although a <u>lack of positiveness</u> is a fact to be <u>considered by the jury</u> in determining the <u>weight of the evidence.</u> (<u>People v. Strollo,</u> 191NY42,62, 83NE573). But a witness cannot testify to a <u>mere impression</u> as to the identity of a person (<u>People v. Williams,</u> 29Hun520; <u>People v. Moulton,</u> 21N.H.586). A witness may state whether a photograph or a bust is a good likeness. (<u>Schwartz v. Wood,</u> 21NYS1053)"(emphasis supplied). (<u>Richardson</u> on Evidence, 8th Ed., sec. 384 et seq. p. 367).

G. <u>IDENTIFICATION - HOW ESTABLISHED?</u>

Many methods are employed in establishing identity. These are by the use of non-scientific methods, such as observations by sight, and admissions and confessions; scientific methods, such as fingerprinting, and methods that are a combination of both, such as photographs, sight recognition, plus fingerprints, and circumstantial evidence.

Identification is a question of fact for the jury (People v. Mezzapella, 19AD(2)729; People v. Tobin, 27AD(2)954).

> NOTE: in homicide cases, the fact of death of the person alleged to have been killed must be proved by direct evidence. Identity of the dead person and the agency of the defendant as the one who killed the person, as alleged, must be proved beyond a reasonable doubt (People v. Palmer, 109NY110).

H. SIGHT RECOGNITION - PSYCHOLOGICAL FACTORS.

One would think that identification resulting from face-to-face observation would be not only the simplest method of establishing identity but also the most accurate. Unfortunately, this is far from the truth. Even persons trained in observation err. A dozen people observing the same incident will give a dozen different versions as to what occurred, - a fact readily attested to by judges, lawyers and psychologists.

When one unexpectedly finds oneself involved as the victim of, or witness to, a crime, the shock, excitement and psychological reaction of victim and witnesses alike, play havoc with perception, recall, recollection and accuracy of description of the events with particular reference to an accurate description of the culprit or culprits involved.

"Testimony concerning events witnessed just once is highly inaccurate. Some of the reasons for this inaccuracy are: incorrect observation, variations in interests and attitudes, unintentional elaboration in 'recall', forgetting, and response to suggestions, such as are involved in questions designed to aid recall, or, at times, to mislead the person making the recall." ("Psychology," Munn, Bowdoin College, page 169).

"Accuracy of recollection . . . Most legal testimony by witnesses of accidents and crimes is based on incidental memories. Thus gross inaccuracies are likely to appear in the testimony, a fact which should be kept in mind by those involved in a legal trial." ("Introduction to Psychology," Boring, Langfeld, Weld, p. 359).

"A flood of imagery arises when an individual is faced with a problem, that is to say, with a relatively new situation for which he has no habitual response. Let stimuli call out conflicting reactions, and doubt arises as to a course of action, and thereupon many images will be experienced. These images represent possible ways of solving the problem. They symbolize modes of action or facts previously learned and now of possible use in a new situation." (Boring, Langfeld, Weld, ibid. at p. 374).

Thus, error, often tragic, is due to imperfect recollection, defective perception and suggestion.

"Testimonial evidence as to identity thus brings up the whole question of possible errors in Perception, Recollection and in Narration, due to suggestion." (3Wigmore on Evidence, sec.786a, p.164). Suggestion, like the "leading question," taints the identification and weakens the weight of the identifier's testimony.

Sight Recognition

We perceive things through stimuli. The stimuli induce perception "when the individual is already prepared or primed to perceive" (<u>Boring, Langfeld, Weld</u>, ibid., pp. 413-414). Such preparation or priming is hardly to be anticipated in one who unexpectedly finds himself the victim of or witness to a crime.

"Under our rules of evidence a witness is competent to testify if he possesses three testimonial attributes: power to perceive what goes on around him, the capacity to remember what he has perceived, and finally, ability to articulate these impressions in an intelligible fashion. As is well known, only a minimal capability to perform these functions is essential to competency, and the witnesses' limitations affect the weight rather than the admissibility of his testimony.

* * * * *

"The crude psychology of a century ago which distinguished between a perception and a judgment, the former connoting the physical act of sensing data from the outside world, the latter the intellectual process of organizing those data, seems to be preserved only in the trial of a lawsuit. Every perception is an act of judgment, as Santayana has observed. The patent conflicts in testimony of eyewitnesses make this dramatically apparent. Absent the head-on collision between two witnesses, however, we are prone to overlook the inherent weaknesses of all perceptions . . . What we see is a function of what we are. The human organism by nature seeks harmony with its environment. If a perception upsets the balance, the mind will reshape the perception until it is more comfortable with it.

10

*   *   *   *

"The same drive for intellectual harmony recurs when a witness is asked to recall what he has seen or heard. No one is satisfied with half a perception, and, faced with this, the mind naturally rushes to fill the void with what should have been there. Of course, each of us has his own notion of what should have been there, and, accordingly, the gaps will be filled with details which our own environment suggests. . .

"Environment also lends meaning to indifferent acts. If a small dot moves across a screen, followed by a larger dot, many witnesses will state that the larger dot is 'chasing' the smaller. If the dots are reversed, they will see the large dot as 'leading' the small one. The implications in a murder case where two men have been seen on a dark street are obvious.

"Even in articulating our ideas, psychological gremlins are at work. Like it or not, a witness feels an allegiance to the side which has done him the honor of calling him to testify, and no matter how well-intentioned he may be, unconscious bias creeps into his testimony. The adversary atmosphere pervading the courtroom and the natural nervousness which comes to a witness who suddenly finds himself occupying stage center do not materially aid the quest for dispassionate truth."

The ". . . perceptions and recollections of witnesses are the playthings of psychology. . . ." (McLaughlin, Book Review - Marshall: "Law and Psychology in Conflict," New York Law Forum, Vol. XII, Number 4, p. 703).

Sight Recognition

I. SIGHT RECOGNITION - PHYSICAL FACTORS.

1. THE FACE AND HEAD. Identification by sight usually is done by recognition of facial and head features. Identifying witnesses should be examined as to the following items pertaining to the face: color of skin, shape of face, e.g. cheekbones, proportions of face, nose, eyes and their color, expressions on face, marks, scars, blemishes, ears, hirsute adornments and color, hair on head or absence of same, eye glasses if any and type worn, tattoo markings (People v. Marrero, 23AD(2)546, aff'd 16NY(2)994).

2. GENERAL APPEARANCE - COLOR AND RACE. In addition to facial and head features, examination of identifying witnesses as to general appearance of the accused is relevant. These include height, weight, manner of walking (his gait), any deficiency of legs or arms, pigeon-toes way of walking, any limp in walking, posture in standing or walking.

The color and race of the accused, as described by the witness, is particularly important where, for example, the witness is a white man and the accused is a Negro. It is believed by many, that members of the white race have difficulty in distinguishing one negro from another. "The inability of ethnologists to agree on standards for classification of humans into ethnic groups, especially in the areas of pigmentation, lends weight to this thesis. (See Encyclopedia Britannica, Fourteenth Ed., Vol. 18, p.865 et seq, "Races of Mankind").

Wall in "Eye-Witness Identification" quotes Mr. Justice Frankfurter as being of the same opinion. (See Frankfurter "The case of Sacco and Vanzetti)."

Although this point has been argued with some success in some cases (<u>People v. Burris,</u> 19AD(2) 557), it has not as yet received the seal of approval in New York (<u>People v. Hunter</u>, 20NY(2)789). In <u>Burris,</u> "Both the Court and the assistant district attorney suggested to the jury that the identification of the defendant by the complaining witness should be weighed in the light of the fact that both the defendant and the witness were Negroes. We have firmly rejected the weighing of testimony on the basis of racial similarity or dissimilarity of witnesses (<u>People v. Hearns</u>, 18AD(2)922)."

In <u>Hunter,</u> the defendant urged in the Court of Appeals that the trial court should have permitted him to argue the question of identification before the jury where racial dissimilarity existed, as to the reliability of complainant's identification of the defendant, the former being a white man and the latter a Negro. In his concurring opinion, Judge Van Voorhis, restated the rule in <u>Burris</u>, and added "there is no general rule or presumption that it is more difficult for a witness to identify members of another race than his own, and we do not regard it as a proper subject for expert testimony." Many modern psychologists will disagree and would extend the issue to include Asiatics as well as Negroes (Wall, ibid, at page 122).

Nevertheless, Judge Van Voorhis did recognize the existence of the problem and added "Upon the other hand, defense counsel should not have been precluded from cross-examining the complaining witness concerning whether he, individually, encounters difficulty in distinguishing between members of the defendant's race." (Hunter, ibid, at page 709).

J. THE INTERESTED - BIASED WITNESS,

Marshall's statement ibid, "like it or not, a witness feels an allegiance to the side which has done him the honor of calling him to testify . . . and unconscious bias creeps in," must not be overlooked when cross-examining a witness for either side. Among our many psychological quirks, unconscious partisanship on the part of the "mere" witness is one of them.

Questions put to such a witness, insinuating his bias or partisanship - his "allegiance" to the side that called him as a witness - will often elicit remonstrances that he is not biased. In many cases, such remonstrances will be in tones so strong or vehement, as to indicate to the jury that he is in fact a partisan and is an "interested" witness.

1. THE "INTERESTED" WITNESS. "Generally, the interest of a witness, as affecting his credibility, signifies the specific inclination which is apt to be produced by the relation between the witness and the facts in issue in the litigation, and connotes or implies concern for the advantage or disadvantage of the parties to the cause . . . The test of interest is to be applied to all witnesses, and, while the circumstances may vary, the test remains the same, and where witnesses of apparently equal credibility disagree, circumstances tending to indicate which version of the transaction is reliable will be care-

fully considered." (98C.J.S.sec.538, p. 475 et seq.).

2. THE BIASED WITNESS. "A biased witness is one who has a motive to color his statements, to suppress the truth, or to state what is false. While pecuniary interest of the witness is the most common source of bias, close relationship to the party for whom he testifies, hostility to the opposite party, or any other circumstance which, according to common observations and experience, tends to create a partisan feeling, also give rise to bias. (98C.J.S.538, p. 475 et seq.).

The testimony of an interested witness should be carefully scrutinized. A police officer may be an interested witness. His zeal in his work, his desire for approbation from his superior officers, his desire for a promotion, are elements which should be probed to determine if he is an interested witness (People v. Moyer, 186AppDiv278, 283).

A witness' testimony may be attacked to show interest, motive or bias (Valdez v. United States, 244US432; Whartons Criminal Law Evidence, 3rd ed., sec.746; People v. Katz, 209NY311).

"Testimony from an interested witness need not be believed and cannot be accepted as conclusive." If he is an interested witness, that fact can be shown as reflecting on his credibility. (98C.J.S.539). In criminal law "In determining the weight and sufficiency of the evidence to establish particular facts or to sustain conviction or acquittal, matters. . . such as the fact of the witness being . . . interested in the result, should be taken into consideration." This is a question of fact

Interested Witness

for the jury (23C.J.S.905, p. 541).

"The testimony of interested witnesses, such as near relatives, interested persons, and those testifying in their own behalf, should be carefully scrutinized and should not be given the weight of testimony of disinterested witnesses, and if there is anything affecting its credibility it cannot be accepted as conclusive, especially where it is contradicted by circumstances in evidence, or by testimony of other witnesses, or where it is self-contradictory or equivocal; but if the testimony of such a witness, or any part thereof, is worthy of belief it is entitled to the same weight as if he had no interest." (23C.J.S.905, p. 544).

"It is true, . . . that the trier of the fact is not required to accept the uncontradicted testimony of a witness, particularly where he is an interested party . . . However, a corollary of this rule is that the uncontradicted testimony cannot arbitrarily be rejected." (Ramsey v. United States, 263F(2)805,807; People v. Kovach, 7Misc(2)542,166NYS(2)659).

Note, a prosecution witness' testimony as to identity requires no corroboration, even if he is the sole witness for the People. (23C.J.S.905, p.544).

K. JURY CHARGE - INTERESTED WITNESS.

A jury charge which stated that "The defendant is an interested party, he is interested in the result of this trial, and the interest of a witness is always to be considered by the jury on the question of credibility as a witness, especially where he is contradicted by other witnesses. A witness who has no interest whatever in the

16

outcome of a lawsuit, who is entirely disinterested, other things being equal, is entitled to very much more credence than a witness who is interested in the verdict of the jury. Especially is that so where the witness is contradicted by other witnesses," was held to be an erroneous charge. The Court of Appeals held:

"A disinterested witness is not, necessarily, entitled to any more credit than an interested witness. The whole subject of the interest of the witness and its effect upon his testimony is for the jury." (People v. Gerdvine, 210NY184,186).

And note, in People v. Noblett (96AD293,295-296), the court said: "The court did not err in refusing to charge that, 'in estimating the value of (the witness) - they should consider that he has a motive to testify, a strong motive, in that he has . . . two civil suits pending against the defendant in which he will probably be a witness and the defendant will be a witness.' It will be observed that the request is not to charge that the witness had a strong motive to testify untruly or adversely but that he had a strong motive to testify - whatever this may mean . . . the court could not, as a matter of law, instruct the jury that he had a strong motive, nor could it be assumed that the defendant would be a witness in the civil actions."

Set forth below is a typical jury charge on "Interested Witnesses," as pertaining to criminal prosecutions:

INTERESTED WITNESSES

"When considering the credibility of each witness, you have a right to see whether that witness

17

has any interest in the result of the trial, and if you find that a witness has such interest, you may bear that fact in mind when weighing his or her testimony. You may consider whether or not that interest has in any way colored his or her testimony so as to misrepresent the true version of the facts.

"Of course, an interested witness is not necessarily entitled to less credit than one who is disinterested, but you have a right to search the evidence for those facts from which you can reasonably conclude that the interest of the witness may have in some way affected his or her credibility. As I have already indicated, it is for you to determine the extent of the interest a witness may have in the outcome of the trial, and thus be better guided to measure the degree of credence or reliability to be given to his or her testimony. Whether or not any witness who has testified in this case has any such interest is for you to determine, in accordance with the rules which I have herein explained. The defendant, as a matter of law, is an interested witness, and I so charge you.

"It is quite clear that the defendant in every criminal case is an interested witness, because upon the result of the jury's verdict may rest consequences unpleasant to him if the verdict is one of guilt. The law does not say, however, that for that reason the testimony of the defendant should be disregarded; because, if that were true, it would be useless for any such defendant to take the witness stand and testify in any court in his own behalf." (<u>People v. Lucas</u>, County Court, Kings Co., April 4, 1962).

L. THE INTERESTED - BIASED WITNESS - CROSS EXAMINATION.

Many avenues of cross-examination are open. Since money is the root of all, or, most evils, the victim of a robbery or burglary may have a financial interest at stake - such as, an insurance policy against money losses, health insurance policy which provides for regular payments during periods of incapacity. He may have a civil suit pending for damages, especially in cases involving automobiles (not limited to personal injuries). Assault cases fall into the same areas.

"Is the witness related by blood, friendship, or business connections with the complainant? Is the witness an "enemy" of the person "against" whom he is testifying - has he had occasion to testify against or speak unfriendly of him?"

Is the witness a member of some law enforcement agency, or related to someone who is? Police, lawyers and the like have formed certain bias, unconsciously, in cases of crime. Other professional men, such as doctors, have certain prejudices in their field of endeavor.

The witness who volunteered his name to the police or to the victim may have some inner compulsions, which should be explored. As an example, some people like to see their names in the newspapers.

The possibilities of racial and religious prejudice and bias, as well as personal animus, should not be overlooked.

An alert attorney will often see openings made by the witness during his direct examination that should be exploited.

1. <u>THE COACHED WITNESS</u>. In the usual court case, we find that much reliance must be placed on the "sight recognition." To establish or destroy the identification thus attested to, is the function of the prosecutor or defense attorney, respectively. The strengths and weaknesses of face-to-face recognition and observation must be explored.

No trial lawyer worth his salt would enter a courtroom without proper preparation. To most laymen, a trial is an unusual experience. Many persons feel that "lawyer's tricks" will be employed to entrap them. The experienced trial lawyer is aware of this. He must prepare his witness to answer questions truthfully. It is surprising how often a complainant or a defendant, when asked "did you discuss the case with your lawyer before coming to court?" will answer "no," - a palpable misstatement which he knows to be untrue. It is this sort of thing, among others, that requires trial preparation.

Awareness of the tricks that memory plays also requires a rehearsal of the facts involved in the case. (<u>Munn</u> supra; <u>Boring, Langfeld, Weld</u>, supra). Rehearsing the facts and coaching the witness are two different things. It is an old saying that it takes a genius to lie consistently. If the witness has been coached, or there is a suspicion of that fact, cross-examination is required as to what suggestions may have been made to the witness, if any, which has led to his testifying to certain facts. (See discussion of <u>Wade</u>, <u>Gilbert</u> and <u>Stovall</u>, infra.) The cross-examiner should explore into the time lapse between the commission of the crime and the date of the trial; the witness' physical condition at the time of the incident; lighting conditions; his position at the time (was he standing, or on the ground, was his back to the culprit, how long did he actually have him under observation); how many times did he confer with his lawyer (or the district attorney as the case may be) prior to the trial; did he confer with witnesses, and if so, how often; what description of the culprit did he give to the police and when; how does that description fit the defendant; did he identify any other person as the culprit; did he ever tell the police he could not recognize or identify the culprit; had he been drinking prior to the incident; does he wear glasses.

2. CROSS EXAMINATION. Cross-examination of the complainant might disclose that he is suing the defendant civilly for damages. This factor should not be overlooked.

One other matter should be borne in mind. Some trial lawyers do not go over the trial testimony with their clients in person. They leave this chore to a trial preparation man. The witness in such a situation is then in a position to state on the witness stand that he never spoke to the trial attorney about the case. The reverse is also true. Some trial lawyers may ask the witness "did you ever see me before this date?" and get a "no" as a truthful reply.

"Few are the criminal actions in which an attempt is not made on cross-examination to impair the creditibility of key witnesses for the prosecution." (People v. Caserta, supra, at p. 25).

Based on the psychological factors mentioned above, the field for cross-examination on identity is broad indeed.

A good trial lawyer makes fairly certain that he knows what the answer will be before he puts the question. In criminal cases, information is usually available to him from the police, police records and the complainant himself as to many areas which he desires to explore on cross-examination. For instance, he should readily ascertain if the witness wears glasses, or whether he appeared to be intoxicated at the time, the lighting conditions at the time of the incident, etc.

M. CHILDREN AS WITNESSES.

Various states have various rules with respect to corroboration of testimony of children.

The imagination of children and their easy suggestibility is well-known. In New York, testimony of children under 12 who were sworn would be considered in the same light as that of any other witness (People v. Palladino, 237NYS(2)266). Although this is theoretically correct, appellate courts are reluctant to affirm convictions based on the child's testimony alone- especially that of the younger teen-agers.

Of course, no conviction can stand on the uncorroborated and unsworn testimony of a child under 12 years (CCP sec. 392).

It is also to be noted that under the Revised Penal Law of New York convictions for sexual offenses will not be valid on the uncorroborated testimony of the victim (N.Y. Penal Law Sec.130.15), sexual abuse in the third degree (P.L. 130.55) excepted.

In cases involving children – infant complainants – more especially those involving charges of sexual abuse, but not limited to those cases, the presence of the parents at the identification of the suspect, and often in court while the child is testifying, is highly undesirable. It is conducive to erroneous identification. Frequently the child will repeat, consciously or otherwise, what he thinks it would please his parent to hear. The child wants to put his best foot forward. If he lied to his parent, or had been involved in some mischief he did not want the parent to know, he would normally be reluctant to disavow the lie in the presence of the parent, either at the lineup or on the witness stand.

Most children have vivid imaginations. Play-acting, aided and abetted by the comics, T.V. and the movies, plays a large part in their lives. They are highly suggestible and easily led.

"Children, being obviously less critical than adults are more suggestible; as a consequence, their testimony is particularly untrustworthy." (Boring, Langfeld, Weld: "Introduction to Psychology," p. 275).

The "only" child and the lonely child develop this trait to an even greater degree.

"Children who are left too much alone invent imaginary playmates to help fill their solitary hours, even though they do not realize their need for companionship. When they are mistreated by a servant or a teacher, the images of their dreams and daydreams

23

represent ways of getting rid of the offending person."
(<u>Boring, Langfeld,Weld</u>, ibid. p.376). Of course, although
<u>Boring</u>, <u>Langfeld</u> and <u>Weld</u> mention only "servant and
teacher" those terms must be synonymous with any adult
who mistreated them or whom they think treated them
unjustly.

N. <u>IDENTIFICATION - QUESTION OF FACT FOR THE JURY</u>

The credibility of a witness on the question of
identification is one of fact for the jury to determine.
Courts are reluctant to hold that identification testimony
of a witness is unbelievable as a matter of law. A
case in point is <u>People v. Regina</u> (19NY(2)65,69-70).

In an appeal from a murder conviction, appellants
urged that the testimony of one Anthony Getch,
a witness for the prosecution, was unbelievable as
a matter of law.

The witness, <u>Getch</u>, testified that at 1:30 P.M.
he was riding as a passenger with the deceased
and one other along a highway in Suffolk County
when another automobile carrying three persons
pulled alongside on the right and began firing pistol
shots into the car driven by the deceased. <u>Getch</u>
testified that he was in the front passenger seat
and that, in the few seconds before he ducked
under the dashboard, he observed the other car
alongside and saw <u>Regina</u> driving, pointing and firing
a pistol. He also saw two other persons in <u>Regina's</u>
car, one of whom he recognized as <u>Battista</u>, also an
appellant. The entire period of observation during

which Getch observed Regina and Battista was no more than 4 or 5 seconds. When Getch sat up and looked again, the other car was gone.

"According to the appellants, it is inconceivable that during the 4 or 5 second period Getch could have seen all of the following: (1) Regina, driving with one hand and pointing the pistol with the other, looking at Getch and at the road ahead, while Getch, throughout, was looking at Regina, at Regina's gun and at everyone else in the auto; (2) that another man was next to Regina whom Getch did not recognize but that he kept his eyes on this person too at all times; (3) that Battista was sitting in the back seat and that he, Getch, observed him throughout; (4) that, during a part of this time, Regina's vehicle was within 2 feet of the vehicle in which he was riding, and (5) that Getch waited until 2 shots were fired before ducking down . . ."

The credibility of this testimony was for the jury to determine. "There is nothing inherently inconceivable or even unusual about the above testimony by Getch. Common experience dictates that a person can observe an entire scene or more than one person at a time, especially where the grouping is within the narrow confines, such as an automobile."

There are situations where the action is so intense and vivid that things seen are burned into the mind. Some psychologists, as noted above, would not be in accordance with this belief. Yet, in spite of scientific experiments in this area of observation and recall, the courts are inclined to let the jury determine this issue. After all, it is a question of fact, and as to factual questions the jury is the sole judge (Cf. <u>People v. Strollo</u>, supra; <u>People v. Moulton</u>, supra).

Hypothetical questions put to an expert witness may be so worded as to likewise invade the province of the jury as to the determination of the identity of the defendant.

Thus, in <u>People v. Buffington</u> (AD(2) ,287NYS (2)243), the Court held that permitting the prosecution to ask a hypothetical question involving the request for an opinion of a Medical Examiner as to whether acts of the defendant, or acts of the principal witness for the State caused death was prejudicial error where issue of the identity of the killer or killers was extremely close.

In this case, the hypothetical question of seven pages in length which favored the State's version of the crime was put to the witness. "All of this not only invaded the province of the jury but was seriously prejudicial. The issue of the identity of the killer or killers, as stated, was extremely close. Faced therewith the jury may well have cast the opinion of this doctor and public official on the scales against appellants upon the mistaken notion that he knew something about the case that they did not."

O. <u>SCIENTIFIC METHODS OF IDENTIFICATION</u>.

1. <u>FINGERPRINTING</u>. The fingerprint is the best and most scientific method of identification. J. Edgar Hoover, Director of the FBI, has recommended that everyone should be fingerprinted for that purpose alone, if for no other (Pamphlet Vol. 152, Library, City Bar Assn., N.Y., "Problems of Identification," <u>Hoover</u>).

The system of fingerprinting was devised by Sir Francis Galton, based on the theory of J.E. Purkinje advanced in 1823 that one's fingerprints never change. They persist throughout one's lifetime.

Fingerprints consist of whorls, loops, ridges, arches, and composites, and are classified accordingly, for ready reference. The use of fingerprints for identification purposes is of ancient origin. Rulers in the East used it to authenticate documents and as their signatures. Fingerprints make identification prompt, inevitable and absolutely accurate. The same is true of human footprints, to some extent. New-born babies in large metropolitan areas are foot-printed and fingerprinted for identification (Encyclopedia Britannica, 14th Ed., Vol. 9, p. 249).

Although Purkinje advanced the theory and Galton

devised the system of fingerprints, it was Mark Twain who instructed the public at large in the physical basis of the system by putting a thumb mark (fingerprint) in "Pudd'nhead Wilson"

"I beg the indulgence of the court while I make a few remarks in explanation of some evidence which I am about to introduce, and which I shall presently ask to be allowed to verify under oath on the witness-stand. Every human being carries with him from his cradle to his grave certain physical marks which do not change their character, and by which he can always be identified - and that without shade of doubt or question. These marks are his signature, his physiological autograph, so to speak, and this autograph cannot be counterfeited, nor can he disguise it or hide it away, nor can it become illegible by the wear and mutations of time . . . this signature is each man's very own - there is no duplicate of it among the swarming populations of the globe!

"This autograph consists of the delicate lines or corrugations with which Nature marks the insides of his hands and the soles of his feet . . . these dainty curving lines lie close together, like those that indicate the borders of oceans in maps, and . . . they form various clearly defined patterns, such as arches, circles, long curves, whorls, etc., and that these patterns differ on the different fingers. . . . The patterns on the right hand are not the same as those on the left . . .. The patterns of a twin's right hand are not the same as those on his

27

left. One Twin's patterns are never the same as his fellow-twin's patterns . . . You have often heard of twins who are so exactly alike that when dressed alike their own parents could not tell them apart. Yet there never was a twin born into this world that did not carry from birth to death a sure identifier in this mysterious and marvelous natal autograph. That once known to you, his fellow-twin could never personate him and deceive you."

A more accurate dissertation on fingerprints would be hard to find. Yet, this is a quotation from "Pudd'n head Wilson" Chapter XXI, written by Mark Twain, almost 100 years ago. It epitomizes the whole valid basis of fingerprint identification. Puddinhead Wilson had his subject run his fingers through his hair. The natural hair and scalp oils adhered to the subject's fingers in sufficient quantity to make a "fingerprint" possible, when the tips of the fingers were pressed on a small glass slab. Hair oils were the precursors of fingerprint ink, according to Mark Twain.

There are occasions when latent fingerprints are left behind by a criminal although such instances are very very few. There are other occasions where the facts disclosed that, fingerprints were left or should have been left on items which came into the possession of the police immediately after the commission of the crime and where the police failed to "dust" the items for fingerprints. This latter situation was argued most effectively in the first trial of People v. Bianculli (9NY(2)468) which ended in a hung jury.

The reliability of fingerprints is thus available for conviction or acquittal if properly used.

2. <u>BLOOD SEROLOGY AND BLOOD GROUPING</u>. In cases where blood is involved, analysis thereof may lead to identification, when compared to the blood of the suspect. Taking of blood samples by a licensed physician, over the protests of the subject, is not violative of the privilege against self-incrimination under the Fifth Amendment (<u>Schmerber v. California,</u> 384US747).

Blood groupings used for purposes of blood transfusions, to-wit, "A", "AB", "BA" and "O", are not too helpful for identification purposes. The more highly sophisticated blood groupings into Rh factors are highly satisfactory and accurate for this purpose, especially in disputed paternity cases (<u>Schatkin;</u> "Disputed Paternity Proceedings", Chapt. IX).

Examinations of blood may also result in identification or in any event may constitute an element of circumstantial evidence.

Blood tests are used in disputed paternity proceedings and in assisting identification of a suspect as the perpetrator of a crime. "The legal value of the evidence afforded by this (blood grouping test) is acknowledged because it is based on facts scientifically and objectively established." "(Paternity Blood Grouping Tests, <u>Schatkin,</u> (NYC Bar Assn. Library pam. vol. 1488, pt. 8); <u>Schatkin,</u> "Disputed Paternity Proceedings", p. 164 et seq.)

Scientific Methods

Modern medical science has identified 90 different sorts of human blood. These run the gamut from the more common types as A, AB, O, B and M-N types to the rare types of Rh^1, Rh^{11}, Rh1 and Rh2.

In forensic medicine the ability to analyze and identify the blood group of a blood sample is of immense importance. Fresh blood is the easiest to test accurately. If wet blood stains are found at the scene of a crime and are promptly brought to a laboratory for analysis, identification of the blood group is comparatively simple.

Dried blood is much more difficult to analyze. In members of the white race, certain secretions, such as saliva, nose secretions and semen, will accurately disclose A or B blood type in 85% of the cases.

Determination of the blood group of the sample analyzed (blood or secretion), when compared with the blood group of the suspect's blood, will, if different, exclude him as a suspect and will result in his discharge. However, even if the blood of the sample and the suspect are found to belong to the same group, the suspect may still be innocent because many individuals have the same blood type. Nevertheless, such similarity of the blood type is an element of circumstantial evidence which may be considered by the jury on the question of identity as well as guilt. (<u>Wiener</u>: "Forensic Importance of Blood Grouping," (NYC Bar Assn Library Pam., Vol. 1681, sec. 10, p.44)).

a. <u>Disputed Paternity Proceedings</u>. In disputed

paternity proceedings, blood group tests are admissible for exclusionary purposes only.

In blood groups there is a causative relation between the traits of the parent and the offspring. The "blood-composition of a child may be some evidence as to the child's paternity. But thus far this trait . . . can be used <u>only negatively</u>, i.e., to evidence that a particular man P is <u>not</u> the father of a particular child C." (<u>Wigmore</u> on Evidence, 3rd ed. sec. 165a; <u>Schatkin:</u> "Disputed Paternity Proceedings," supra, chapts. VII, VIII; Family Court Act, sec. 532).

"The defendant's right to the (blood test) is a substantial one, and it is mandatory upon the Court to grant it." If the defendant is indigent, the expense of the test must be borne by the County. The blood test must be demanded before the trial of the paternity suit. (<u>Schatkin:</u>"Disputed Paternity Proceedings," p. 194).

b. <u>Cross-examination</u>. It is not a matter of common knowledge that only a few medical men are proficient enough today in making an accurate blood analysis, particularly with respect to the Rh factors. It is therefore of extreme importance to examine the medical expert most minutely on his expertise in this regard. Conceding the doctor's expertise in regard to his ability to analyze blood is not advisable unless counsel is most certain of the man's qualifications.

Other items for cross-examination in blood

test identification are indicated in the foregoing

(1) Was the blood sample fresh or dried blood.

(2) Method and means of transporting the blood sample to the laboratory for analysis, including the time element.

(3) How was it received and where was it stored, and for how long a period of time, before it was analyzed. Was it refrigerated.

(4) Chain of possession at laboratory - could the sample be confused with other samples submitted or on hand in the laboratory for analysis.

(5) Except in paternity cases, how many other persons have the same blood grouping as the defendant.

3. <u>MICROSCOPY - MICROSCOPIC INVESTIGATION</u>. Identification of small particles of organic matter (e.g. skin, hair, nail parings, etc.), fibers of all kinds, including cloth as well as inorganic matter, is often helpful in identifying persons and things.

Modern science has made great strides in this field since the development of the simple, compound microscope and ultra-microscope.

What is "seen" under the microscope will often depend on the equipment used, the way in which it is used, and the skill of the miscroscopist. Improper illumination of the microscope slide for example, will give a false reading. "If, therefore, a particle is large enough, or a fibre is thick enough, to send sufficient light up into the object-glass, the particle will be seen as a bright disk, or the fibre as a bright line of light extending much beyond its apparent end as shown by transmitted light." (Encyclopedia Britannica, supra, Vol. 15, p.446).

This illustration should be sufficient caution to counsel to be prepared throughly before cross-examination of a microscopist is undertaken.

Ballistics testimony is largely based on microscopic examinations. Pathological examination, including microscopy, of hair, skin and nails may also be employed for identification purposes.

Similar examinations of other items where relevant, such as narcotics, cloth, etc., have been made with important effect. It is to be noted, however, that in certain instances a search warrant must be obtained to seize the items to be examined. Absent a search warrant, or a search incident to a lawful arrest, or a showing that the item seized had been abandoned, a timely motion to suppress and exclude such evidence at the trial would be granted (State v. Miller, 206A(2)835; Fahy v. Connecticut, 375US85; Abel v. United States, 362US217; Preston v. United States, 376US364; Cooper v. California, 386US58; Ringel, "Arrests, Searches and Confessions," page 179 et seq.; cf. Schmerber v. California, supra).

4. VOICE IDENTIFICATION - TELEPHONE. A layman may give his opinion as to identification of a person by his voice (Wilbur v. Hubbard, 35Barb(N.Y.) 303). The person engaged in a telephone conversation or listening in on it, may testify as to the conversation providing he can identify the voice on the other

end of the telephone. "If a witness knows the speaker and recognizes his voice, all cases agree that the evidence is admissible. (Murphy v. Jack, 142NY216." See also People v. Levis, 96Misc513,529, 161NYS824; Rimes v. Carpenter, 61Misc614, 114NYS96; People v. McDonald, 177AppDiv806, 165NYS41).

"A witness may also testify to a telephone conversation with a person whose voice he did not know at the time but which he subsequently recognized as the voice of the speaker whom he met thereafter. Such evidence may be weak, but it is, nevertheless, admissible. People v. Strollo, supra (191NY42,62); People v. Dunbar Contracting Co., 215NY416,422,109NE554" (Richardson on Evidence, Seventh Ed., sec.524, p.468).

In summary, voice identification as a result of a telephone conversation is admissible if the witness participated or listened in on the conversation, providing he knew the person speaking, either before or after the conversation, and recognized (identified) his voice.

Where an issue is raised as to whether an eavesdropper-witness was able to hear words allegedly spoken, as for instance, in an adjoining room, evidence of experiments conducted by others, to this effect, have been held admissible (State v. Ratkovich, 111Mon.19, 105P(2)679).

"A condition of sound may be evidenced by instances of other persons' experience in hearing under similar conditions." (Wigmore on Evidence, Third Ed., sec.460, p.485).

TELEPHONE OR ELECTRONIC EAVESDROPPING ADMISSIBILITY.

If the voice identification took place as a result of a wiretap or electronic eavesdropping ("bugging"), the admissibility of such identification in evidence would be subject to the proscriptions of the Fourth Amendment.

In Berger v. New York (388US41), the United States Supreme Court held that the New York wiretap section (C.C.P. sec.813-a), which authorized ex parte wiretap orders, was unconstitutional. Evidence of identification, as well as other evidence obtained thereby, would be inadmissible. However, the New York Court of Appeals revived section 813-a by its decision in People v. Kaiser (21NY(2) 86).

If the evidence were obtained by the use of an electronic eavesdropping device, it would be inadmissible unless a lawful order, following certain well-defined guidelines, had been followed. (Katz v. United States, US , 36L.W.1091; Osborn v. United States, 385US323; People v. Kaiser, 21NY(2) 86; Intercepting Telephone Communications, 284NYS (2)431; People v. Scharfstein, 52Misc(2)976, 277NYS (2)516).

5. VOICEPRINTS AND VOICEGRAPHS. The study of the physics of sound has resulted in the development of scientific devices to make voice identification possible.

Sound is caused by energy. This energy sets air particles in motion, resulting in a back and forth movement of the air particles which continues until the imparted energy is exhausted. In simple sound-producing instruments, such as a tuning fork, the movement of the air particles, called sound waves, can be measured graphically. The resulting graph represents a simple <u>sine</u> curve. (<u>Boring, Langfeld, Weld,</u> supra, pp. 561-562).

The new devices make "voiceprints", and, like fingerprints, identify the person involved. Just as fingerprint identification uses the unique features of the fingerprint, the whorl, ridge and loop, so voice print identification uses the unique features in the "spectographic impressions of peoples' utterances of 10 commonly used English words, <u>the</u>, <u>to</u>, <u>and</u>, <u>me</u>, <u>on</u>, <u>is</u>, <u>you</u>, <u>I</u>, <u>it</u>, <u>and a</u>."

The voiceprints can be recorded on paper and show the resonance bars (bar voiceprint) and contour voiceprint, which measures the level of loudness. The loudness (volume) level appears on the voiceprint like contour lines on a topographical map.

By examining the bars and the contours, the voiceprint of the speaker can be identified. They have proved 99% accurate.

Attempts to disguise the voice by whispering, muffling the voice, or holding the nose, do not alter the basic identifiable features in a person's voiceprint. "Voice mimics and ventriloquists were also unable to prevent proper identification of their voices. It is believed that each voice is uniquely different enough to make them identifiable with the same accuracy that fingerprint identification enjoys."

This claim is based on the mechanism of speech.

Voiceprint uniqueness is determined by the vocal cavities and articulators in the human body, to wit, the throat, nasal cavity, the two oral cavities, tongue, lips, teeth, soft palate and jaw muscles.

"The claim of voice patterns' uniqueness rests on the improbability that two speakers would have vocal cavities' dimensions and articulator use patterns identical enough to confound voiceprint identification methods." The voiceprint identifier has been used in courts in White Plains, N.Y., Stamford, Connecticut, and Los Angeles, California, in cases involving sales of narcotics and obscene telephone calls. (Connecticut Bar Journal, Vol, 40, p. 586, (Dr. Lawrence G. Kersta), Dec. 1966). (People v. Straehle (Westchester County Court) The New York Times, April 12, 1966; United States v. Wright (Travis A.F.B.), San Francisco Chronicle, May 27, 1966; Connecticut v. Modugno (Stamford Advocate), July 2, 1964; California v. King (Los Angeles Times), June 2, 1966).

A similar device was used in a case in New Jersey. In that case the defendant was directed to submit to a tape recording of his voice for the purpose of comparison with a graph prepared from a recording in the possession of the prosecutor's office. Among the objections raised by the defendant were, the use of the instrument itself, violation of the Fifth Amendment, and violation of fairness and justice (due process) under the Fourteenth Amendment. The Court disposed of these various contentions as follows:

The burden of the State to produce evidence to convict does not limit the State in its use of new devices representing swift strides in the fields of technology and science. In this case "The accused is merely required to speak into a microphone of a device capable of recording the sound of his voice, the voice, like fingerprints and facial features, being distinctive from individual to individual. It is a clearly distinguishable physical characteristic. Additionally, the defendant may use any words on any subject and may not be required to make any reference to the acts surrounding the indictment. Clearly this is as objective as a fingerprint and should be considered accordingly." (State v. McKenna, 226A(2)757,760).

Directing a defendant to submit to this type of test in a criminal proceeding would not violate the defendant's privilege against self-incrimination under the Fifth Amendment.

Voice identification tests and examinations have been sanctioned for some time. These tests were conducted by the simple method of compelling a defendant to speak while within hearing distance of the victim or a witness to the crime and having either of them state that this was the voice he heard at the time in question. Today, a voice graph has been developed, which is one step further than auditory identification.

a. Admissibility. Voice identification is a certain type of examination or inspection which is out-

side of the scope of the Fifth Amendment
privilege against self-incrimination. It is non-
testimonial in character and is equated with
other tests such as fingerprinting, photographing, examination of the body of a person for
identifying characteristics, drunkometer tests
and blood tests, all of which may be compelled
without violating the self-incrimination statute.
Such a test does not constitute "testimonial or
communicative compulsion." (Schmerber v. California, 384US757; Holt v. United States, 218US
245; State v. King, 209A(2)110; 8 Wigmore on
Evidence (McNaughton Rev.Ed.) sec.2265, pp.
395-96).

Nor does the type, nature and method of
administering this voice test violate the sense
of justice and fairness implicitly guaranteed in
the Federal Constitution, e.g. the Fourteenth
Amendment. (See Rochin v. California, 342US
165).

Nevertheless, the weight and effect of any
scientific evidence such as this is still for the
jury to determine. (State v. McKenna, 94NJ
Super71, 226A(2)757).

b. Voiceprint-Voicegraph, Cross-Examination.
Cross-examination of witnesses as to the accuracy of voiceprint identification would be
indicated as to the following areas:

(1) Were the 10 "test" words, mentioned above,
used in the identification process. Can they
be confused with other similar sounding

words. Did the subject speak with a foreign accent; if so, the effect thereof.

(2) The effect of surgery, if any took place, on the suspect's nose, antrim or sinus cavities, lips, jaw, tongue, throat, jaw muscles or soft palate. Had any of these organs been injured (e.g. fractured nose or jaw).

(3) Did the suspect have any false teeth or dentures and have any of them been replaced or repaired. Or has the suspect lost any teeth before the test was applied.

6. THE AUDIOMETER. One's ability to hear may be of some importance in identification (see State v. Ratkovich, supra; Wigmore, supra, sec. 460, p. 485). An audiometer is a device used to test one's hearing ability. Many people experience some difficulty in hearing sound within normal decibel ranges. Some fail to hear the low decibel sounds, and some the high decibel range. When necessary or advisable, a hearing test of a witness should be conducted on the audiometer, which produces a graph showing the range, in decibels, of one's hearing ability. This graph is called an audiogram.

"An audiograph is a graph showing the relation of audibility to frequency . . . An audiometer is used in making such a graph. An audiometer is an instrument by which the power of hearing can be tested and measured."

An audiogram is not a record kept in the ordinary course of business. The accuracy of an audiogram "depends upon the trustworthiness of the scientific device used in making them and the skill of the person who operates the instrument."

These machines must be tested frequently. The tests must be conducted in sound-proof rooms, for accurate results. The areas of cross-examination are obvious (Quadlander v. Kansas City Public Service, 224SW(2)396, 400, 401).

7. X-RAYS. A body which has a degree of radio-opacity or opaqueness will show in an X-ray unless it is screened out by some other radio opaque substance. In other words, it cannot be relied upon, in all situations, to show everything.

"The best known property of X-rays . . . is their ability to penetrate substances quite opaque to ordinary light, but it must not be thought that all X-rays are equally penetrating . . . Certain rays are able to penetrate several centimeters of steel while others are stopped by a few millimeters of air." (Encyclopedia Britannica, 14th Ed. Vol. 23, pp. 840,845).

Improper use of X-rays causes loss of hair (depilation) (Encyclopedia Britannica, ibid., at p. 846), a fact which should be noted in the area of identification.

Of further importance in the use of X-rays in the field of identification is the ability of the rays to detect faulty castings, forgings, metal welding, and the detection of paintings which have been painted over by other paintings. Modern pigments are, in general, less opaque to X-rays than the

pigments used many years ago. X-rays will therefore detect "hidden" paintings. It is apparent that
other forgeries, e.g. documents, can be disclosed
by the use of X-ray techniques. (Encyclopedia
Britannica, ibid., p. 847).

These properties of X-rays should not be overlooked when examining witnesses with reference
to the identification and genuineness of documents
and similar items.

The term "photograph" as applied to X-rays
is a loose term. Actually the X-ray plate is a
negative which shows shadows. A print may be
made from this negative. The print is called the
positive or photograph, though this is seldom used.
The negative itself is all that is required for diag-
noses and interpretation.

It is invaluable in showing bullets and metal
fragments imbedded in one's body. Dental work and
tooth structures are also readily disclosed by X-ray.
Old fractures show up - a very important item in
identification.

In cases involving a shooting, locating the bullet
in one's body enables it to be extracted. Proper
ballistic examination in some cases would materially
assist in identification.

Many persons have been identified by comparison
of their tooth structure with X-rays taken in the
normal course of dental care by one's dentist.

After the proper foundation has been laid, X-ray
pictures, if relevant, are admissible in evidence.
"X-ray photographs are received in evidence be-

cause the instrument used in taking such pictures is known to be a trustworthy one . . . In order to render an X-ray picture admissible, the proponent must first establish the accuracy of the photograph by showing, among other things, that such picture was made by a trustworthy instrument, and was properly taken by a person qualified for that work; and he must verify the identity of the person or object whose condition is in issue . . . III Wigmore Evidence, sec. 795 . . . The sufficiency of the verification of an X-ray picture is within the discretion of the trial judge." (Quadlander v. Kansas City Public Service, 224SW(2)396).

It will be noted that the basis for introducing an X-ray photograph into evidence parallels that which is required for the introduction of still pictures and moving pictures. However, in X-ray photography, there are some major differences which may require extensive cross-examination or examination on a voire dire.

There was a time in medical practice, at least, when only medical doctors took X-ray photographs - the medically qualified M.D. - the roentgenologist. Today, specially trained X-ray technicians, many of whom are registered nurses, do the actual picture taking. In any event, cases involving the human body, such as identification, physiological conditions, injuries, etc. would almost always require a medical doctor for a proper interpretation and for establishing identity. Cross-examination of the X-ray technician as to his qualifications would seem to be indicated.

Furthermore, most X-ray negatives are stamped with a file number only, for purposes of identifying the person whose X-ray has been taken. Error in record keeping, an item which requires exploration in the court, might easily result in identification error.

Additionally, X-ray machines are much more intricate and sophisticated than cameras. They are also more sensitive to movement. This is due to the relatively slow speed of the emulsion which requires a relatively long time for adequate exposure. The slightest movement, even breathing, while the picture is being taken, blurs the outlines in the X-ray picture and this will be readily apparent on the plate.

X-ray pictures are also used to photograph objects. The physical structure of some objects may defy X-ray photography. Such objects are radiolucent.

8. IDENTIFICATION BY FOOTPRINTS. A description of the length and breadth of footprint tracks, the marks left by the sole of the footwear worn, and whether the toes of the wearer turned in or out, may be given by a witness who saw them. A comparison between the tracks seen by the witness and those made by the suspect may be presented to a jury for its determination as to whether both set of tracks were made by the same person. Admittedly this is not an easy question to resolve

(Hotchkiss v. Germania Fire Ins. Co., 5Hun.90 (N.Y.)).

The public interest in obtaining evidence "far outweighs by a clear margin the private interests sacrificed" when a suspect is required to do certain purely physical acts, such as putting on shoes or rolling up his sleeve.

"In this category a variety of concrete cases have been ruled upon as not covered by the Fifth Amendment privilege.

* * *

"2. Imprinting of other portions of a suspect's body (e.g. foot in mud, nose and cheek on window) for purposes of identification."
(8 Wigmore on Evidence, sec. 2265, pp. 386-399.)

9. THE BERTILLON SYSTEM OF IDENTIFICATION. This system known as anthropometry, was the first scientific system devised for identification. It was invented by the French savant, Alphonse Bertillon, the handwriting expert, who testified in the notorious Dreyfus case. The system which bears his name was described in his Photographie Judiciaire (1890).

Although the Bertillon system is no longer in use due to its costliness, the lack of superior skill found in the lower police echelons and the large margin of error implicit in the system which resulted in many failures in identification, the basic elements of the system are set forth, since they present a good guide for examination and cross-examination of witnesses where identification is in issue.

The system encompassed the following:

a. <u>Descriptive data.</u>

(1) Complexion, color of hair and eyes, shape of nose, ears and face, absence of hair, hirsute adornments.

(2) Special body marks - moles, tattoos, scars, skin blemishes.

(3) Body measurements - height (standing and sitting), reach of the arm, length and breadth of the head, length of the right ear, breadth of the cheek.

(4) Extremities - length of left foot, length of left middle finger, length of left forearm and hand.

(5) Habits - gait while walking, handwriting (compare Wade, Gilbert, Stovall, infra), preferences, accomplishments, voice, personality.

(a) Talking - gestures, if any, shrugging of shoulders, touching people while talking, facial motions while talking.
(b) Clothing - type usually worn, hands in pockets.
(c) Eating habits - table manners, drinking habits at meals.
(d) Nervous habits - facial twitching, tic, blinking of eyes.
(e) Speech - fast, slow, loud or soft, taciturn or voluble, use of profanity.
(f) Voice quality - rasping, basso, pitch, lisping, stammering, stuttering, foreign accent, regional accent, use of foreign phrases.

(g) Style of speech – grammatical, cultured, profanity, choice of vocabulary.

(h) Appellation – nick-names, aliases.

Note: J. Edgar Hoover, Vol. 152, supra, says that a man may use many aliases in his lifetime, but a nickname stays with him forever. It is his "monicker", his label.

b. Interests and Tastes. His favorite subject of conversation, knowledge or ignorance of certain subjects, knowledge of foreign languages, sports skills, artistic ability (music, painting etc.), professional accomplishments.

c. Handwriting Exemplars and Enlargements. Comparisons – taking an exemplar of a suspect's handwriting is not violative of the Fifth Amendment (Schmerber v. California, supra; Holt v. United States, 218US245).

Enlargements of handwriting exemplars, like photographic enlargements (see Cowley v. People, 83NY464) are also admissible. However, in Cowley, the court held that where the original exemplar was not produced in court and where, in addition, the enlargement was of poor quality, the enlargement was inadmissible – "incompetent." (Cowley cited Hynes v. McDermott (22 Al. Law Journal 368) as authority.

Although Bertillon is credited with devising anthropometry, he was in fact preceded by Leonardo da Vinci (1452-1519), a man of great intellectual curiosity. Da Vinci's many excellent anatomical plates have not been surpassed. He made a study of facial muscles in laughter, tears, and anguish. He watched men being executed in order to record their facial muscle reactions for later delineation.

"To be able to recall these faces, he thought of a method, which anticipated the Bertillon system now used in legal medicine, based on a division of noses into straight and curved, the straight into short and long, with round or pointed extremeties, and the curved noses into three groups according to the curvature. These divisions and subdivisions were given numbers; all he had to do therefore to be able to recall a face later on was to jot down the numbers that stood for the chacteristics of the nose, mouth and eyes."

(M.D. Medical Magazine, Vol. 11, No. 8, August 1967, p.16).

10. <u>OTHER SCIENTIFIC METHODS OF IDENTIFI-CATION</u>. Science has developed techniques in reconstruction of various parts of the body which result in fairly accurate approximation of the original. This is particularly true in skull, bone and teeth reconstructions. The resulting effect is to present a good description of the person involved.

Footprints which leave marks or impressions on surfaces have also been used to determine the height of man (by the length of the stride), as well as any defect of the individual's legs or feet by the evenness or unevenness of the footprint. (As to resemblance and comparison of footprints see <u>Hotchkiss v. Germania Fire Ins. Co.</u>, 5Hun90).

P. NON-SCIENTIFIC METHODS OF IDENTIFICATION.

   1. PHOTOGRAPHY. When the Chinese philosopher said that a picture is worth a thousand words, he was, of course, referring to a true and accurate picture. Photography is widely used today for identification purposes by both public and private investigators. The photographs may be "stills" or motion pictures. A clear, bright "still" such as police department "mug shots" are good evidence of identity.

   However, photographs can be "doctored." The negative can have lines added or obliterated to change, modify or alter the appearance of the subject. This is called "retouching" and is a common practice among professional photographers who wish to produce a print that is more flattering to their customers. A minute examination of the negative, usually by a magnifying glass, will readily disclose such "retouching".

   Even without altering the negative, changes in a photograph can be accomplished by "magic" in the dark room. In printing a negative, especially under an enlarger, certain areas in the negative can be blocked out very easily. The result is that only a particular portion of the negative will appear in the print (the picture). Shading - holding back light from the enlarger to the print - has a similar effect. This results in either heavy shadows in some areas of the picture or brighter light in other areas.

   The distance between the subject and the

camera at the time the picture was taken is also important. Usually, unless a telescopic lens has been employed, the further the distance, the less the resolution of the picture. This may make identification more difficult. Additionally, use of such lenses creates distortion of the picture, due to spherical or chromatic aberration, particularly toward the edges of the picture. However, enlarging of the picture (the "blow-up") may solve this problem.

How successful the "blow-up" is depends on the type of film used, and the paper on which it is printed. Often, when high-speed film is used, the enlarged print will be granular. This may affect identification. Likewise, if the print is made on "artistic-type" paper, often granular in surface, some distortion may result. For a clear print a "glossy" type paper as opposed to a "matte" type gives the best picture print.

The use of flash-lights and flood lights also present problems, especially in the creation of shadows on the subject's face - and sometimes blinking of the eyes.

Motion pictures present an additional problem. This concerns itself with the speed at which the pictures were recorded - normal (16-18 frames per second), slow motion or rapid (Keystone cop chases). The speed can vary from 8 to 48 frames per second.

Color photography presents other problems. Prints of color negatives do not usually present accurate color reproductions. This may be due to the emulsion on the negative itself, or in the printing of the picture. The print must be made at certain controlled temperatures with little variation allowed. The same is not true of "black and white" pictures. Accordingly, color prints may often show darkened areas where none existed, or show greater or even less intensity in color, or "off-color," that was not present in the original.

Filters are often used in taking black and white pictures. (Only "haze" filters are used to produce natural color in color photography.) Filters vary from white (used to cut haze), to red, blue, green, and yellow-green. Generally, a red filter absorbs blue and green rays and transmits red rays; a yellow filter transmits yellow, green and red rays; yellow, orange and red filters make blue skies look darker. "When shadows are illuminated by light from a blue sky, a sky-darkening filter will also darken shadows. . . A filter may tend to increase the number of tones or shadows of gray which film can produce in a print or subject that has the same color as the filter. . . . A color separating filter can be used for increasing the contrast between colors of almost equal brightness." (G.E. Photo Data Book, p.59.)

The lighting conditions under which the photograph was taken will play an important part in the "accuracy" of the resulting print. High-speed film available on the market today permits photography in darkened areas, due to the high emulsion speed of the negative. Some enlargements of high-speed negatives show granulation on the print.

To get a good picture, there is no substitute for controlled lighting and posing of the type used in police "mug" shots. The full face and side view of the subject, employed in taking these pictures, reduces the error of identity to a minimum.

From the foregoing discussion, it must be evident that a photograph may be so made as to misrepresent the object photographed. It can falsify just as much, and no more, than the person who takes it or verifies it. (<u>Wigmore</u> on Evidence, 3rd ed., sec. 792, p. 185).

2. <u>PHOTOGRAPHY CROSS EXAMINATION</u>. When photographs are used for identification purposes, the following areas may be explored in relation thereto.

a. The time, place and conditions under which the picture was taken.

b. The type of camera (especially lens and lens speed) which was employed.

c. Distance at which subject was photographed.

d. Was the negative doctored.

e. Is the picture a glossy print.

f. Was the print "doctored" in the dark room in enlarging it.

g. Were flash-lights or flood lights employed.

h. Emulsion speed of the film.

i. Was a filter used - what type.

j. In motion pictures - speed at which scene

was taken.

k. In color photography - get details of conditions of printing the picture in the dark room - temperature, etc.

l. In all cases - consider examination of the photographer and the person who developed the negative and who made the actual prints.

3. PHOTOGRAPHS - ADMISSIBILITY IN GENERAL.

"Properly authenticated photographs are admissible in evidence whenever it is competent to describe the physical characteristics of a person, place or thing. (Cowley v. People, 83NY464,476, 38Am.Rep. 464; People v. Webster, 139NY73, 83, 34NE730). Photographs are properly authenticated by the testimony of one or more witnesses familiar with the subject portrayed, that the photograph is a correct representation or good likeness of the person, place, object, or condition sought to be described. (Alberti v. New York, Lake Erie and Western R.R.Co., 118NY77,88, 23NE35, 6L.R.A.765). The testimony of the photographer who took the pictures has been held a sufficient authentication (Cowley v. People, supra." (Richardson on Evidence, sec.672, p. 592).

Thus, in attempting to identify a person by photograph, a witness must testify that (a) he is familiar with the person shown on the picture and (b) that it is a good likeness.

If there is any suspicion that the print (picture) has been doctored in any way, the individual who developed the negative and the person who printed the picture should both be examined. In any event, the negative itself should be scrutinized for signs of alteration. The photographer is always a prime witness.

Any modification by the witness of either statement (a) or (b), ibid, may render the picture inadmissible. Frequently in cases involving pictures of persons who have suffered some facial or similar injury, the witness will state, in effect, "I know him, and that is a good picture, but he was much worse than the picture shows." The latter statement might render the picture inadmissible since it would not be a good likeness of the person at the time sought to be described or referred to. (People v. Caserta, 19NY(2)18,21).

A photograph is a pictorial communication of a qualified witness. Like a map, it is usually more accurate than words. When used as the witness' expression of the thing observed, its use is entirely proper (Wigmore, supra, sec.792, p.178).

However, if the fact that the picture seeks to prove is irrelevant, then the photo itself is inadmissible. This "objection of irrelevancy is commonly either that the condition of a place or person at the time of taking the photograph is not evidence of the condition at the time in issue . . . or that the outward appearance of a person is not evidential of his inward condition." (Wigmore, ibid., sec. 792, par. (1), p. 184; People v. Caserta, supra.)

As pointed out above, a photograph must be verified by some witness as a true representation

Non-Scientific Methods

of the person or object. The witness himself need
not be the maker or the taker of the picture. "He
affirms it (the picture) to represent his observations
and this is the essential element." (Wigmore, ibid.,
sec. 794, p. 188; Boyle v. Ward, 39 F.Supp.545,
549; Kortz v. Guardian Life Ins., 144F(2)676,679).

As the court said in Kortz, ibid., "A photograph
is admissible when it is shown that it is a correct
likeness of the person or objects which it purports
to represent, which fact may be shown by the person
who made the photograph or by any other competent
witness." In Kortz the "other witness" who was
present at the time the pictures were taken testified
fully as to the circumstances. His testimony, it was
held, was a sufficient basis for admitting the pictures
into evidence.

Generally, the "question of sufficiency of preliminary proof to show the correctness of a photograph rests largely in the discretion of the trial
court." (Kortz, ibid., at p. 679).

To the same effect, see Boyd v. Ward, supra.-
"It is not necessary to call the photographer to
prove a photograph of an object. The testimony of
anyone familiar with the original and with the
photograph as a correct likeness of the original is
competent to prove the likeness." (Boyd., ibid., at
p. 548)

The same rule applies with respect to the admissibility of moving pictures. In a negligence
action wherein plaintiff testified that since being
injured he could not go up a ladder, the court

55

properly admitted moving picture film showing plaintiff on a ladder, after one who made the picture identified the film, in order to show plaintiff's ability to work and as bearing on his credibility.

"After the witness who operated the camera properly identified the film and the plaintiff present in court as the person whose likeness appeared in the film, its portrayal to the jury was proper both as to the plaintiff's ability to work and as bearing on his credibility." (Haley v. Hockey, 199Misc512, 103NYS(2)717, 719)

4. PHOTO ENLARGEMENTS. A photographic enlargement is also admissible. "In this day and age when the art of lensmaking has arrived at a state of substantial accuracy, it would be legal quibbling to say that by the magnifying process and the printing thereof on paper that it would tend otherwise than to disclose a correct reproduction, and the court was correct in admitting the" photo enlargement. (In Re Roberts Estate, 3NW(2)161,165-166)

"Judicial notice will be taken of the process whereby photographs are produced. Similarly, the courts will recognize that all civilized communities rely upon photographic representations for presenting resemblances of persons and animals or scenery and all natural objects." (21NY Jur. sec. 79)(Cowley v. People, 83NY464)

Photographic pictures when shown to be correct resemblances of the persons or things represented are competent as evidence.

"A portrait or a miniature taken by a skilled artist, and proven to be an accurate likeness, would be received on a question of identity or the appearance of a person not producible in court. Photographic pictures do not differ in kind of proof from the pictures of a painter. They are the product of natural laws and a scientific process. It is true that in the hands of a bungler, . . . the result may not be satisfactory . . . The portrait and photograph may err, and so may the witness. That is an infirmity to which all human testimony is lamentably liable . . . But where care is taken . . . the picture produced may, in many of the issues for the jury, be an aid in determination."

The same is true as to enlargements and copies of a picture (<u>Cowley v. People</u>, ibid.)

5. "<u>MUG</u>" SHOTS. Care should be used in seeking to introduce photographs of people in evidence, even where they are admissible. As an example, a "mug shot" (police rogues gallery picture) are taken in full face and profile, and are printed on the same sheet for ready identification. They are readily recognizable as such. Introduction in evidence of such a picture of the defendant in a criminal trial has been held prejudicial, even when the bottom of the picture has been taped over to obliterate any reference or indication of the fact that it was a police rogues' gallery picture. Seeing this type of picture alerts the jury to the fact that the in-

dividual has been in trouble with the police before (<u>Barnes v. United States</u>, 365F(2)509; <u>People v. Caserta</u>, supra).

6. <u>COMPOSITE SKETCHES</u>. For the purpose of aiding in the identification of an individual where no photograph is available, police department artists draw a composite picture of the person involved, based on his description supplied by various witnesses. These composite sketches are surprisingly accurate and copies are transmitted to interested agencies to facilitate the apprehension of the individual. They are admissible in evidence on the same theory that renders photographs admissible (<u>People v. Peterson</u>, 25AD(2)437; 266NYS(2)884; <u>People v. Jennings</u>, 23AD(2)621).

> The "Image-Maker". Detective Peter Smith of the New York City Police Department has speeded up daVinci's system of identification (supra) with his invention of the "Image-maker." This machine is a slide projector which flashes images on a screen. It utilizes some 150 slides, each of which depict various facial features. These slides are coded. A witness gives his description of the wanted person to the machine operator. The operator likewise codes the description. By coordinating the coded slides with his coded information, he projects various slides on a screen. By skillful use of the slides, pushbuttons and mirrors, the operator obtains, on the screen, a good likeness of the person

Non-Scientific Methods

described. This process takes about 20 minutes as compared to 4 hours required by a police artist to get the same results.

The time saved by this machine is often critical in apprehending a criminal. ("Spring 3100," June 1963, Vol. 34, No.6, p.3)

7. PHOTOGRAPHS AND COMPOSITE SKETCHES - ADMISSIBILITY. Under New York law, photographs and composite sketches of a defendant may not be received in evidence as part of the People's case unless the identification of the defendant is attacked as a recent fabrication. Under those circumstances the pictures may be introduced to bolster the identification testimony.

Section 393-b, of the New York C.C.P. states:

> "Testimony of previous identification. When identification of any person is in issue, a witness who has on a previous occasion identified such person may testify to such previous identification."

A positive identification of a defendant as the person who committed a crime does not require corroboration. (People v. Dorner, 25AD(2)552, 267NYS(2)634). It is only when such identification is attacked that evidence of corroboration is admissible. Section 393-b, ibid., provides the method by which this may be done.

The rule is that identification by a witness may not be bolstered by the introduction of hearsay testimony. For example, a witness may not testify that a third party identified the defendant as the culprit. Thus, it was error to permit the arresting officer to testify to prior identification of the defendant by the complaining witness (People v. Herrmann, 9NY(2)665,666; People v. Cioffi, 1NY(2) 70,73; People v. Trowbridge, 305NY471,476-477; People v. Altintop, 13AD(2)508; People v. DeJesus, 11AD(2)711,712; People v. Lyles, Jr., 23AD(2)500).

Photographs and composite sketches are pictures made by third parties. They are also hearsay evidence when offered to identify the defendant (People v. Hagedorny, 272App.Div.830; 70 NYS(2)511; People v. Coffey, 13AD(2)410, rev'd 11NY(2)142; People v. Jennings, 23AD(2)621; People v. Singer, 300NY120, 123; People v. Peterson, 25AD(2)437, 266NYS(2)884). Thus, where a photograph of the defendant was admitted in evidence on direct examination of People's case before any attempt by defendant to impeach the witness, its admission was error as there was no evidence that the witness had on a previous occasion identified such person (People v. Hagedorny, supra).

To recapitulate, it is error to permit a witness to testify as to prior identification of the defendant by others. (People v. Mantesta, 27AD(2)748; People v. Allen, 26AD(2)573; People v. Jenkins, 24AD(2)716). Indirect testimony as to prior identification of the defendant by a third party is also improper. Thus, testimony by a detective of conversation had with the defendant wherein the detective told the defendant he had been identified as perpetrator of the crime was held improperly admitted since it was not previous identification by the detective of the defendant. "Although the detective did not testify directly with respect to previous identification of the defendant, he, in effect, did so by relating the conversation above quoted." (People v. Gould, 25 AD(2)160; People v. Sullivan, 5AD(2)847) (See also People v. Trowbridge, 305NY471; People v. Cioffi, 1NY(2)70; People v. Sarra, 283AD876, aff'd 308NY 302; People v. Oliver, 4AD(2)28, 163NYS(2)235, aff'd 3NY(2)684; People v. Ciavarella, 27AD(2)937).

Similarly, the Appellate Division, Fourth Department, held that receipt in evidence of testimony by police officers as to identification of defendant at police headquarters by complaining witness on personal confrontation was error. (People v. Lawrence, AD(2) , 287NYS(2)579).

It is likewise error to permit witnesses to testify that prior to the trial they had identified a photograph of defendant as perpetrator of the crime (People v. Cioffi, supra; People v. Giamario, 20AD(2)815, aff'd 15NY(2)939; People v. Hunnicutt, 15AD(2)536; People v. Mezzapella, 19AD(2)729; People v. Jones, 28AD(2)1087).

These errors are compounded where the issue of identification is close, even if there was no objection made by the defendant (People v. Hoban, 28AD(2)562; People v. Jones, supra). The errors are doubly compounded when the prosecutor makes reference in his opening statements with respect to these illegal identifications (People v. Mantesta, 27AD(2)748; People v. Jones, supra).

The use of photographs by the police in obtaining

identification of the suspect by witnesses is summarized by the United States Supreme Court in Simmons v. United States, decided 3/18/68, as follows:

"It must be recognized that improper employment of photographs by police may sometimes cause witnesses to err in identifying criminals. A witness may have obtained only a brief glimpse of a criminal or may have seen him under poor conditions. Even if the police subsequently follow the most correct photographic identification procedures and show him the pictures of a number of individuals without indicating whom they suspect, there is some danger that the witness may make an incorrect indentification. This danger will be increased if the police display to the witness only the picture of a single individual who generally resembles the person he saw, or if they show him the pictures of several persons among which the photograph of a single such individual recurs or is in some way emphasized. The chance of misidentification is also heightened if the police indicate to the witness that they have other evidence that one of the persons pictured committed the crime. Regardless of how the initial misidentification comes about, the witness thereafter is apt to retain in his memory the image of the photograph rather than of the person actually seen, reducing the trustworthiness of subsequent lineup or courtroom identification.

"Despite the hazards of initial identification by photograph, this procedure has been used widely and effectively in criminal law enforcement, from the standpoint both of apprehending offenders and of sparing innocent suspects the ignominy of arrest by allowing eyewitnesses to exonerate them through scrutiny of photographs. The danger that use of the technique may result in convictions based on misidentification may be substantially lessened by a course of cross-examination at trial which exposes to the jury the methods potential for error. We are unwilling to prohibit its employment, either in the exercise of our supervisory power or, still less, as a matter of constitutional requirement. Instead, we hold that each case must be considered on its own facts, and that convictions based on eyewitness identification at trial following a pretrial identification by photograph will be set aside on that ground only if the photographic identification procedure was so impermissibly suggestive as to give rise to a very substantial likelihood of irreparable misidentification. This standard accords with our resolution of a similar issue in _Stoval v. Denno_, 388US293,

301-302, and with decisions of other courts on the question of identification by photograph.*" (emphasis supplied).

8. EXCEPTIONS TO HEARSAY RULE IN IDENTIFICATION ISSUES. Section 393-b, C.C.P., supra provides that when identification is in issue a witness who has identified the person on a previous occasion, may so testify at the trial. (People v. Siegel, 4AD(2)680; People v. Sarra, supra; People v. Trowbridge, supra). Also, under the well-established hearsay rule "where the testimony of a witness is assailed as a recent fabrication, it may be confirmed by proof of declarations of the same tenor before the motive to falsify existed." (People v. Singer, 300NY120,123). Thus, a composite sketch drawn by a police artist from description by the

---

* "The reliability of the identification procedure could have been increased by allowing only one or two of the five eyewitnesses to view the pictures of Simmons. If thus identified, Simmons could later have been displayed to the other eyewitnesses in a lineup, thus permitting the photographic identification to be supplemented by a corporeal identification, which is normally more accurate. See P. Wall, Eye Witness-Identification in Criminal Cases 83(1965); C. Williams, Identification Parades, 1955 Crim.L.Rev.525,531. Also, it probably would have been preferable for the witnesses to have been shown more than six snapshots, for those snapshots to have pictured a greater number of individuals, and for there to have been proportionately fewer pictures of Simmons. See Wall, supra, at 74-82; Williams, supra, at 530."
(Simmons v. United States, US , 36L.W.4227).

witness given two months before the defendant was arrested was properly admitted into evidence where defendant attempted to show that the witness' identification of defendant was recent fabrication, even though "Ordinarily . . . the sketch . . . would be considered hearsay and could not come into evidence." (People v. Coffey, 11NY(2)142,145; People v. Peterson, 25AD(2)437; People v. Marrero, 23 AD(2)546; cf. People v. Jennings, 23AD(2)621; People v. Hagedorny, supra).

The same rule applies to photographs, based on the same rationale and authorities, ibid.

Other records, such as contemporaneous notations made by a police officer are likewise admissible to counter defendant's suggestion of recent fabrication. Thus, in such a situation, it was proper for the People to introduce records made by the police officer immediately following his purchase of narcotics from the defendant containing a description of the defendant's tatoo marks and lameness (People v. Marrero, 23AD(2)546).

However, where hearsay identification testimony has been erroneously received, a guilty verdict will not be set aside where there is overwhelming additional evidence of defendant's guilt. (Sec. 542, N.Y. C.C.P. - harmless error rule). (People v. Milburn, 26AD(2)420, aff'd 19NY(2)910; cf. People v. Caserta, 19NY(2)18,21). (See also People v. Wright, 27AD(2)718; People v. Rivera, 28AD(2) 687; People v. Phillips, 27AD(2)981; People v. Ronzelli, 27AD(2)517).

Non-Scientific Methods

Exhibiting a single picture of a defendant to an identifying witness, prior to a lineup identification by that witness, would taint the lineup identification. (See <u>Wong Sun v. United States,</u> 371US471). Such an act would obviously be highly suggestive and leading. Additionally, introduction in evidence of a "mug" shot or "wanted circular" showing the defendant's picture, absent some provocation, would be prejudicial since it might reasonably be anticipated "to influence the jury by way of showing probable previous reproachable conduct on the part of defendant." (<u>Tucker v. United States,</u> 214F(2)713, 715; <u>Barnes v. United States,</u> 365F(2)509). However there are some situations where such "single" showing of a picture may be justified.

Thus, where the prosecution introduced an eyewitness to a robbery who identified defendant in a police lineup, and on cross-examination, witness was asked if she had been shown a photograph of defendant prior to the lineup and she replied she had seen an FBI folder containing defendant's picture, it was proper for the prosecution to introduce in evidence the FBI "Wanted Circular" which witness had referred to, in order to dispel the inference that the witness had been shown a photograph of defendant prior to the lineup.

Testimony was developed that such "Wanted Circulars" are routinely circulated among Federal Loan and Savings Association members.

"While it would be error to introduce such a Wanted Circular without provocation, or to influence the jury by way of showing probable previous reproachable conduct on the part of the appellant, such was not the purpose here. On the contrary, this evidence was introduced to show that the witness had not been shown a picture of defendant in particular and then taken to a police 'lineup' to identify the person whose picture she had seen. This evidence did show that in the course of routinely passing over a number of such Wanted Circulars, she had identified appellant. It was thus eminently proper for the prosecution thus to dispel the inference raised by this witness' testimony on cross-examination that she had been shown a photograph of appellant prior to the 'line up.' "

(Cf. Wall, "Eye-Witness Identification," supra, p. 88, 89, in which he criticizes the practice in this country of "publishing photographs of accused persons . . . after arrest and before a corporeal identification has been made." Such a practice increases the danger of mistaken identification since the publication of the picture exerts "a suggestive influence upon the witnesses.")

The Tucker decision (1954) seems to have anticipated Wade, Gilbert and Stovall by many years.

A similar question of prejudice, requiring a reversal, was present in People v. Swanson (278 App. Div. 846, 104 NYS(2)400, 401). In Swanson, other factors were present, which require careful note.

"It was established on trial that the infant complainants, when they confronted the defendant within a few hours after the crime was committed, stated that he was not the man who had committed the crime. During the trial there was received in evidence, as tending to identify defendant as the criminal, photographs of defendant taken after his arrest and while he was in custody. Under the circumstances disclosed, the admission of this evidence was erroneous and highly prejudicial."

Some of those additional circumstances were, (a) the infant complainants identified the defendant at a police station, after his arrest, several days after the crime was committed, (b) this was not a line-up identification but a face-to-face confrontation, and (c) the mothers of the infant complainants were the only outsiders present at the confrontation.

Q. SPONTANEOUS IDENTIFICATION.

Spontaneous identification unaccompanied by any suggestive circumstances " 'is by and large the most reliable type of identification' (Wall, Eye-Witness Identification, p. 181,n.2)" (People v. Dorner, 25AD(2)552). In Dorner the complainant spotted and identified defendant as he was walking along the street in the area of the commission of the crime.

R. DISCOVERY AND INSPECTION.

1. MANDATORY DISCLOSURES BY PROSECUTOR RELATIVE TO IDENTIFICATION. It is generally held that where a prosecutor has evidence which will tend to exculpate a defendant or mitigate punishment that may be imposed, he is under a duty to disclose that fact to the defendant before the

trial. Failure to do so is deemed a violation of due process. (Brady v. Maryland, 373US93; Barbee v. Warden, 331F(2)842; People v. Yamin, 45Misc(2)407; People v. Fein, 24AD(2)32, aff'd 18NY(2)162,722, cert. den. 385US649).

"We think that in order for the non-disclosure of evidence to amount to a denial of due process, it must be such as is material and capable of clearing or tending to clear the accused of guilt or of substantially affecting the punishment to be imposed in addition to being such as could reasonably be considered admissible and useful to the defense." (Giles v. Maryland, 386US66).

When there is any doubt as to the admissibility of such evidence or its helpfulness to the defendant, the question should be resolved by the court - not by the prosecutor. (Griffin v. United States, 183F(2) 990).

Conversely, where such evidence is wholly lacking in probative force because of its speculative quality, no disclosure is required by the prosecutor (United States v. Tomaiolo, 378F(2)26).

In Giles v. Maryland, supra, the Supreme Court remanded the case back to the state courts which had denied post-conviction relief to the petitioner. The basis of the remand was that counsel was denied access to police reports containing inconsistent statements by the prosecutrix in her testimony at petitioner's trial for rape, about her subsequent assertion and withdrawal of rape charges against others. Also, at the post-conviction hearing, counsel was not permitted to explore evidence as to her mental condition, suicide attempt and nymphomania.

Obviously, in such a case, proper cross-examination in the areas indicated would bear heavily on the issue of identification.

Similarly, in Miller v. Pate, Warden (386US1), where the prosecutor introduced in evidence a pair of defendant's shorts which he asserted contained blood stains, when in fact he knew at the time that the stains were paint, and which shorts the defendant was not permitted to examine, constituted a deliberate misrepresentation of the truth. Identification of the defendant as the culprit was, in these circumstances, a violation of due process. A state conviction based on such knowing use of false evidence cannot stand. (Mooney v. Holohan, 294US103; Napue v. Illinois, 360US264; Pyle v. Kansas, 317US213; cf. Alcorta v. Texas, 355US28; People v. O'Rourke, NYLJ 12/14/65 p.18/8). Likewise, in New York the court held it was error for the District Attorney not to have notified the defense either before or during the defendant's trial that the robbery victim on the night of the robbery was unable to identify the defendant from a police photograph (People v. Ahmed, 20NY(2)958).

During trial, the prosecutor must reveal to a defendant testimony of a People's witness that is perjured, even if such perjured testimony is elicited by the defense. (People v. Savvides, 1NY(2)554; Napue v. Illinois, supra; People v. Yamin, supra). Disclosure of perjury in a People's witness opens the door for attack on the question of identification via an attack on the witness' credibility.

2. GRAND JURY TESTIMONY. Attack on the credibility of any witness is fair game. Prior inconsistent statements by a witness opens the door wide, to such an attack. Ammunition for such an attack may be found in the testimony of the witness before the Grand Jury. Where the defendant requests the production of that testimony for cross-examination purposes, it must be produced. (Schlinsky v. United States, 379 F(2)735).

3. PRELIMINARY HEARING TESTIMONY. A preliminary hearing as opposed to a grand jury proceeding is a valuable means of discovery for the defendant. If he does not waive it, he is entitled to the hearing within a reasonable time. Habeas corpus is available to him if he is denied the hearing before or simultaneous with the presentation to the Grand Jury (Wheeler v. Flood, 269 F.Supp.194). A defendant is entitled to a copy of the transcript of such hearing. If he is indigent, he is entitled to a free copy as a matter of constitutional right (People v. Jaglom, 17 NY(2)162, 165; People v. Hughes, 15 NY(2)172).

Testimony of the People's witnesses at the preliminary hearing can also furnish leads for cross-examination on the issue of credibility.

4. PRIOR STATEMENTS. Prior statements of wit-

nesses may be examined during trial by the defense for the purpose of impeaching, contradicting or showing subsequent fabrication. This too is a valuable tool for cross examination purposes. (People v. Malinski, 15NY(2)86). The rule applies only to the People's witnesses. The defendant is not entitled to an examination and inspection of any of the defendant's witnesses statements made to the prosecution (People v. Regina, 19NY(2)683).

5. PRE-TRIAL INSPECTION OF DEFENDANT'S STATEMENTS. Where the People have notified defendant that they intend to introduce at his trial statements alleged to have been made voluntarily by him (N.Y. Code of Crim. Proc., sec.813-f), it has been held that he is entitled to a pretrial inspection thereof, where defendant intends to contest their voluntariness (People v. Huntley, 15NY (2)78; People v. Harvin, 259NYS(2)883, 46Misc(2) 417; People v. Abbatiello, 46Misc(2)148, 259NYS(2) 203).

Such discovery and inspection are limited to written admissions and confessions. The right to such pre-hearing discovery is not extended to oral inculpatory statements, whether or not it is alleged to be contained in police notes or memoranda. As to those, defendant, at the time of the voluntariness hearing, "may request the right to inspect them as an aid in cross-examination after testimony concerning the oral testimony has been elicited." (People v. Fowler, NYLJ, 12/29/65, p.17/3; People

v. Riley, 46Misc(2)221).

6. COURT RECORDS. "Files in the possession of the clerk of the Criminal Court of the City of New York, are public records which may be examined by any person unless they have been sealed from public scrutiny by the court or by statute . . .

"Where the defense of a person accused of a crime requires access to public records or even to records sealed from general examination, the right of inspection has a greater sanction and must be enforced." (Werfel v. Fitzgerald, 23AD(2)306, 260NYS(2)791).

This right to inspection presumably applies to other New York State courts. It must be apparent that it is an important right which may be of great value particularly in cases in which informants are alleged to have been used.

7. POLICE PHOTOGRAPHS AND COMPOSITE PICTURES. In Fox v. City of New York (28AD(2)20) the court held that photographs taken by the police in the course of their official duties were public records and subject to inspection. Although Fox involved an accident case and was an Article 78 proceeding, it would seem that the rationale of that case would not apply to criminal proceedings in which the police may, as part of their duties, take photographs (Public Officers Law, sec.66a; Education Law, sec.144).

However, under the Federal Rule (Jencks Act,

18USC3500(e)), it has been held that a composite picture drawn from descriptions of witnesses to a bank robbery does not come within the purview of <u>Jencks</u> as it is not a writing or memorandum. (<u>United States v. Zurita</u>, 369F(2)474(7th Cir.)).

8. <u>EYE-WITNESS - FAILURE TO CALL A WITNESS</u>. Failure of a defendant to call an eye-witness within his control would permit the jury "to infer that the evidence of (the) . . . eye-witness would be unfavorable to a party who voluntarily excluded him from testifying in the case." (<u>People v. Hovey</u>, 92NY554; 131ALR696; <u>People ex rel Woronoff v. Mallon</u>, 222NY465; Cornell Law Quarterly, XXV, p.442). The same rule applies to the People.

9. <u>SUMMARY</u>. Thus, it is to be noted that the defendant has valuable tools to attack identification, by means of attacking the credibility of the People's witnesses through cross-examination of their testimony (a) before the Grand Jury, (b) at the preliminary hearing, (c) prior statements, (d) court records, and (e) police photographs.

S. <u>DISCLOSURE BY GOVERNMENT OF CONTENTS OF "BUGGED" CONVERSATIONS</u>.

Where the prosecution concedes that a defendant's conversations were overheard unlawfully by a "bug," the defendant must be given an opportunity to prove at a hearing before a judge whether any evidence presented

Disclosure by Government

against him at his trial (including identification) was tainted by the use of the illegal "bug." The prosecutor may not decide this issue by himself. The decision is for the court to make. Accordingly, <u>all</u> recordings taken by the Government must be disclosed. (<u>Kolod v. United States</u>, US , 36L.W.3306). See also <u>People v. Miller</u>, 28AD(2)1205, 285NYS(2)495).

T. THE JURY CHARGE ON IDENTIFICATION.

Care must be exercised in charging the jury on identification. The charge on identification which follows, summarizes substantially the elements to be considered on establishing identity:

"Identification of the defendant may be shown through any means by which the individuality sought to be established can be differentiated from that of every other individuality. It is a well-recognized rule that a witness may testify to the identity of a person from any fact that leads him to believe that he knows the identity of such person. <u>Permanency</u> of the individuality is the basis from which the identity of a person is inferred. This not only relates to the physical contours, but includes as well carriage, manner, action, temperament, clothing, voice, and each and every physical and mental characteristic. Each separate element may coincide exactly with that of one or more individuals, but the combined elements mark with certainty the distinction. Because of these elements, identity oftentimes becomes a matter of opinion.

"A witness may base his conclusion on the appearance, size, tone of voice, or mark, or peculiarity of the defendant. Other facts may also be considered for the purpose of identifying the defendant, where evidence shows that a crime has been committed by someone, so that identity becomes the sole fact in issue. The jury should acquit the defendant unless such identification is established beyond a reasonable doubt.

"On the question of identity of the perpetrator of a crime, no precise rule can be laid down, except that the evidence ought to be strong and cogent, and that innocence should be presumed until the case is proven against the defendant in all its material circumstances beyond all reasonable doubt.

"Where a witness identifies a defendant as the man who committed the crime, the weight of the evidence of identification is for the jury.

"The identity of the defendant as the person who committed the crime must be shown with sufficient certainty to preclude a reasonable possibility of mistake.

"The ultimate question of the truthfulness of the witness' statement on identification is for you (the jury) to decide. You have the right to consider all the circumstances under which an identification is made, the opportunity to make it, the power of observation, and generally all the attendant circumstances in coming to a conclusion as to whether or not you accept as a fact the statement that the defendant was the one perpetrating the crime."
(People v. Anderson and Moore (Ringel, J.), aff'd

20AD(2)931).

U. ADMISSIONS, CONFESSIONS AND EXCULPATORY STATEMENTS.

An admission is circumstantial evidence of guilt. A confession is an express acknowledgment of guilt (People v. Bretagna, 298NY323).

An admission, confession or exculpatory statement, lawfully obtained from a suspect, may be sufficient to identify him as the culprit.

It is not the purpose of this treatise to examine the large body of law on this subject. However, it should be borne in mind that the statements of the defendant, including any statement as to his identity in relation to the offense charged, is not admissible in evidence if the "Miranda" warnings had not been first administered (Miranda v. Arizona, 384US436). These warnings are fourfold. They must be given to a defendant if he is in custody. The merger of the privilege against self-incrimination and the right to counsel intimated in Escobedo v. Illinois (378US478) was affirmed in Miranda. By "in custody," the court means that the defendant has been arrested or "otherwise deprived of his freedom of action in any significant way" (Henry v. United States, 361US98). This "arrest" is not limited to custody or detention in a police station. It can occur on a public street. Furthermore, the fact that the police officer intended that the defendant not be permitted to leave is not controlling. The test is whether the defendant believed he was under detention that controls (People v. Rodney P. Anonymous, 21NY(2)1). Purely voluntary statements are not excluded.

Admissions,Confessions,etc.

They do not come within the ambit of the Miranda rules (People v. Torres, 21NY(2)49).

The warnings mandated by Miranda are:

1. defendant has a right to remain silent;
2. he has the right to the aid and presence of counsel;
3. the right to stop talking at any time;
4. if he cannot afford counsel, one will be assigned to him free of charge.

Absent the giving of these warnings, not even exculpatory statements made by the defendant are admissible. The warnings once given need not be repeated (United States v. Gower, 271F.Supp.655).

In New York, a motion will lie to exclude statements made by a defendant if they were obtained in violation of Miranda or were otherwise involuntary (C.C.P. secs. 813-f,813-g).

"Conversations" are things that may be "seized" within the purview of the Fourth Amendment (Katz v. United States, supra). Accordingly, it would seem that they are things subject to suppression (i.e. exclusion) under Fed. R. Crim.Proc., sec.41(e) and New York State rule (C.C.P. secs. 813-f,g).

V. MODUS OPERANDI.

The age of specialization has not bypassed the criminal. Some only commit burglaries of a certain kind, others commit only robberies. Some are experts in forgeries, with their specialties in that field. Some use weapons. Some do not. Some prefer knives and some hand guns. Some prefer the suburbs for their activities and some prefer urban areas. Some deal with drugs and drug addicts and some with homosexuals.

Every modern law enforcement agency carries a detailed dossier on known criminals in which the habits, proclivities and idiocycrancies of each are listed in detail. (See Bertillon system supra). These dossiers are known as the Modus Operandi File. In New York City the abbreviated form of the title is used - the M.O. File. Proper use of the file often enables the police to pin-point the culprit. The British call this "catching a thief on paper." When the M.O. File is supplemented with rogue gallery pictures ("mug" shots) the task of the police is simplified. Though proof of a suspect's prior criminal activities cannot be used to establish his guilt of the particular crime with which he stands charged, (Cf. People v. Molineaux, 168NY264), such knowledge of a suspect's proclivities and patterns of behavior can make the police work of apprehending the suspect so much simpler.

W. SELF-IDENTIFICATION.

In loitering and vagrancy cases failure to identify oneself to a police officer is not a crime (People v. Tinston, 6Misc(2)485; People v. Bomboy, 229NYS(2)323).

A New Jersey statute punishing one as a disorderly person who is apprehended by the police and "cannot give a good account of himself" does not constitute a crime and is unconstitutionally vague (United States v. Margeson, 35L.W.2160 (U.S.D.C.,E.Pa); City v. Forrest (Cleveland Mpl Court), 35L.W.2443).

However, under N.Y. C.C.P. Sec. 180-a, a police officer may require identification of a suspect. The right to inquire is founded in the common law (<u>People v. Rivera,</u> 14NY(2)441).

X. <u>EXPERT TESTIMONY AND WITNESSES</u>.

It is obvious from the references noted above that the use of expert testimony is often necessary to establish identification, either directly or more particularly by circumstantial evidence. (But as to hypothetical question involving identity, see <u>People v. Buffington,</u> supra.)

1. <u>JURY CHARGE - EXPERT TESTIMONY</u>. The law pertaining to testimony by expert witnesses is summarized in the following charge to a jury in <u>People v. Rivera</u> (Ringel, J., 1958, Court of General Sessions):

"The law of this state permits an expert who is skilled in his particular science not only to testify to facts, but to give his opinion upon matters of a scientific nature. This is allowed because an expert is supposed, from his experience, research and study, to have peculiar knowledge upon the subject of the inquiry and he is supposed to be more capable than a layman of drawing conclusions from facts and to base his opinion upon them.

"In weighing the value of an expert's testimony, you should consider the learning, his professional standing, and his opportunity for study as well as his experience.

"It is of great importance that the facts upon which he draws his conclusion should be established to your satisfaction, since a false premise may render such an opinion valueless. The purpose of expert testimony is to aid you in your deliberation as to the particular subject concerning which expert testimony is admissible. But such testimony is merely a guide to you in your deliberation of fact and you, at all times, remain the sole and exclusive judges of those facts.

"Expert testimony should not be accepted or rejected indiscriminately. It is to be weighed and considered by you the same as any other evidence. After weighing and considering it, you are at liberty to disbelieve the whole or any part of it when either improbable or incredible or when you believe that an expert witness has either testified falsely or was mistaken with respect to any material fact or opinion. Then, too, the reasons, conclusions or opinions of an expert are not binding upon you – that is, you do not have to regard them as conclusive – but on the other hand, you have no right to arbitrarily or lightly reject the testimony of an expert, nor should you reject it just because he is an expert."

2. CROSS-EXAMINATION OF "EXPERT WITNESS". In cross-examining an expert several things should be borne in mind. It is basic that the attorney should have knowledge of the subject in question before he embarks on an examination of the witness. "Homework" by the lawyer is imperative.

If the witness is really an expert, conducting a voire dire in an effort to avoid a ruling by the court declaring the witness to be an expert, should be avoided. Invariably, a real expert witness will recite such an impressive personal history regarding his claim to be regarded as an expert that the jury will be greatly impressed by his subsequent testimony. Experience has shown that the really astute prosecutor will not accept defendant's concession that the witness is an expert, but on the contrary, will insist that the witness recite his "expert" background for the benefit of the jury. He wants them properly impressed.

Counsel should not be over-awed by the "expert" witness. Sound pre-trial preparation by counsel should enable him to cope with his testimony. The fact that the witness is a medical doctor does not mean that he is really an expert in all fields of medicine. As an example, the jury will ordinarily not be overly impressed by a doctor who testifies as to a dermatological condition, when his own specialty happens to be ophthalmology or obstetrics. In the medical field, a doctor's specialty is easily verified by reference to the local medical directory, available in any doctor's office, the County Medical Society or public library.

The same sort of reference books are available as to other professions, e.g. lawyers. When the expert is an engineer it should be noted that there are many specialties in this field - civil, mechanical, electrical, etc.

The late Bernard Shaw said "All professions are conspiracies against the layman." Unfortunately, many professional men want to keep it that way. As a result they are often miffed when a mere layman, like a lawyer, should presume to question them as to matters in their particular field of expertise. A show of a dogmatic approach as to his conclusions or a show of irritation by the expert will not be lost on most juries. And, after all, it is for the jury to decide whether to accept or reject the expert's testimony. (See also, Wellman, "The Art of Cross Examination" 4th Ed. p.76 et seq.).

Y. CIRCUMSTANTIAL EVIDENCE.

A photograph of the criminal committing the crime would probably be the best way of identifying him. "The use of photographs for identification purposes constitutes one of the most valuable tools of effective law-enforcement." (Wall, "Eyewitness Identification," p. 89). Many banks employ just such a method by use of hidden cameras. However, every victim of a crime does not go around armed with a camera and in most cases crimes are committed hidden from "the intruding eye." Accordingly, proof of the identity of the criminal often depends on circumstantial evidence.

Richardson, supra, section 111, defines this term as "Evidence of some collateral fact, from which the existence or non-existence of the fact in question may be inferred as a probable consequence . . . Baird v. City of New York, 96NY567, 593."

However, an inference cannot be based upon an inference (People v. Volpe, 20NY(2)9). (Cf. Wigmore, Treatises on Evidence, 3rd ed., sec. 41, who holds to the contrary.)

According to <u>Richardson</u>, ibid. (sec.113, p.89) the rule simply means "that where circumstantial evidence is relied upon, the facts upon which the inference is based must themselves be established by convincing evidence, as distinguished from remote, uncertain, or highly conjectural evidence, and, in a criminal case, 'must be of such a character as, if true, to exclude to a moral certainty every other hypothesis but that of the guilt of the accused.' (<u>People v. Lewis</u>, 275NY33.)"

Although the general rule states that proof of other crimes is inadmissible to prove that the defendant is guilty of the crime for which he is on trial (<u>People v. Goldstein</u>, 295NY61,64), yet "evidence of the commission of another crime is admissible when its object is to prove a motive for the crime charged." (<u>Pierson v. People</u>, 79NY424; <u>People v. Scott</u>, 153NY40; <u>State v. Pancoast</u>, 5ND516; <u>People v. Morse</u>, 196NY306)(<u>Richardson</u>, ibid., p. 122-123). Likewise, evidence of other crimes may be introduced to prove intent - always an essential element to the commission of a crime (<u>People v. Molineux</u>, 168NY297).

Of similar importance, evidence of other crimes is admissible to prove identity. (<u>People v. Hill</u>, 198NY 64; <u>People v. Thau</u>, 219NY39; <u>People v. Jung Hing</u>, 212NY393).

Proof of flight, escape, resistance and concealment is also admissible to prove guilt and, a fortiori, identity. (<u>People v. Yazum</u>, 13NY(2)302; <u>People v. Conroy</u>, 97 NY62, 80). Obvious misstatements are admissible for the same purpose (<u>People v. Brady</u>, 16NY(2)186; <u>People</u>

v. Hook, 15NY(2)776).

Other items of proof are admissible as elements of circumstantial evidence. These can run the whole gamut from proof of the defendant's good character to the deceased's bad character in a self-defense homicide case (Wigmore on Evidence, 3rd ed., sec.51).

These items can include evidence of traits, and skills, mental and physical powers (or lack of same), possession or lack of money, habit, custom, traits of handwriting and spelling, presence of a design or plan, threats and motive. Although motive is always relevant, it is never essential (Kennedy v. People, 39NY245,254).

Opportunity to commit the crime, possession of its fruits, footmarks, blood tests, ballistics reports may also be relevant on the question of circumstantial evidence.

Possession of the fruits of a crime recently after its commission is prima facie evidence of guilty possession, and if unexplained or falsely explained, either by direct evidence, by the attending circumstances, by the habits of life and character of the prisoner, or otherwise, it is sufficient to warrant a conviction by a jury. (Knickerbocker v. People, 43NY177; Greenleaf on Evidence, sec.34; People v. Jackson, 182NY66; People v. Galbo, 218NY283; People v. Berger, 260App.Div.687, aff'd 285 NY811).

However, any and all of these items "are mere circumstances to be considered and weighed in connection with other proof with that caution and circumspection which their inconclusiveness when standing alone require." (Hickory v. United States, 160US408,417).

Thus, evidence of flight or concealment by the

accused is relevant and admissible only if there are facts pointing to the crime charged as the motive which prompted it (People v. Reddy, 261NY479,486; 3Wigmore on Evidence, secs. 276, 1052).

(For areas of cross-examination as to personal elements of identification, such as traits, skills, etc., see Bertillon System, supra).

JURY CHARGE - CIRCUMSTANTIAL EVIDENCE.

An example of an approved charge as to circumstantial evidence follows:

WHAT CONSTITUTES CIRCUMSTANTIAL EVIDENCE?

"By circumstantial evidence is meant proof of facts and circumstances by witnesses who testify to things seen or heard from which inferences can be drawn as to the ultimate fact in issue. It consists of a chain of circumstances so woven link by link, each link into the other, as to lead from the proof of things seen and known one by one down to the establishment of the unknown and unseen fact, the untimate fact in issue.

"Let me give you an example: Let us assume that in a certain case, the issue is whether it rained between sunset and sunrise. An attorney may call a witness to the stand, a policeman or pedestrian, who may testify that after sundown he walked along the streets and that the rains came down and that he saw it and that he felt it and that he perceived it by the use of one or more of his senses. This is eye-witness testimony. This is known as direct evidence on the issue.

"Let us assume for the sake of this illustration that no such eye-witness was available but that in lieu of the testimony of an eye-witness a person testified substantially as follows: that he went to bed at dawn and that the streets were then dry and that there was no rain coming from the heavens, that the houses in the vicinity were all dry and that the leaves on the trees were dry and that the sidewalks were dry. He states he awoke at sunrise and he found that the streets were all wet, that the trees were dripping with moisture much more than dew would normally account for; that the rooves (roofs) of the houses were all dripping and full of moisture. Mind you, at no time did he see the rain come down. He merely testified to the existence of certain circumstances. Would you not think that any sensible jury would have the right using their common sense to come to the conclusion that, by reason of such testimony, they believed it had been raining during the night, although there was no eye-witness to establish it? There you have a very homely example of the difference between direct or eye-witness testimony and circumstantial evidence.

"Now, what is the law with reference to circumstantial evidence? Circumstantial evidence is evidence of facts and circumstances from which the existence of particular facts may be established legitimately and properly.

"In the example I just gave to you, the fact to be inferred was that it had rained between sundown and sunrise, and that inference was drawn from all of the circumstances testified to by the witness who went to bed at sundown and who arose at sunrise and who testified to what he observed when he woke up.

"In an attempt to prove a fact by circumstantial evidence there are certain rules to be observed that reason and experience have found essential to the discovery of proof and to the protection of the innocent. The circumstances themselves must be established by direct proof, and must not be left to rest upon inference. The inference which is to be based upon the facts and circumstances so proved must be clear and strong and logical with an open and visible connection between the facts found and the proposition sought to be proved.

"In determining a question of fact from circumstantial evidence, the hypothesis of guilt should flow naturally from the facts proven. They should be consistent with them all; and the evidence must be such as to exclude to a moral certainty every reasonable hypothesis but that of the guilt of the crime charged against the defendant. Or, in other words, the facts proven must all be consistent with and point only to his guilt and they must be inconsistent with his innocence.

"In considering circumstantial evidence, the jury must not base inference upon inference, but only upon a fact. Now it would serve no useful purpose to indulge in any observations as to which form of evidence is more convincing. If evidence in a given

Circumstantial Evidence

case be so convincing as necessarily to prove a defendant's guilt to a moral certainty, that is, beyond a reasonable doubt, it is of little moment by what kind of proof that guilt is established. If you are so convinced, a verdict is proper whether you are so convinced by direct evidence or circumstantial evidence.

"All that you should be concerned with is whether the evidence in this case satisfies your minds of the guilt of this defendant beyond a reasonable doubt." (Schweitzer, J., People v. Colligan, 12AD(2)449, aff'd 9NY(2)900).

PART II
POLICE LINE-UPS

A. THE FACTS.

A trilogy of cases decided by the United States Supreme Court at the June 1967 term (United States v. Wade, 388US218; Gilbert v. California, 388US263; Stovall v. Denno, Warden, 388US293) has radically altered the rules respecting police lineup or showup identification.

In Wade and Gilbert the suspects were subjected to lineup identifications after indictment and after counsel had been assigned to represent them. The lineups were held on an illuminated stage before an audience of about 100 persons. The stage lights were so arranged that neither Wade nor Gilbert could see into the audience. In neither case were their attorneys notified of the impending lineup nor were they present thereat.

In Wade, the lineup consisted of 6 other persons. All of them, including Wade, were required to wear strips of tape on their faces and to say "Put the money in the bag." Wade involved the robbery of a bank. Two bank employees identified Wade at the lineup as the robber. At the trial, on direct examination, they also identified Wade. Their pre-trial lineup identification was then elicited from them on cross-examination.

In Gilbert a robber used a handwritten note demand-

The Facts

ing money. The police took handwritten exemplars from Gilbert, seized photographs from his apartment unlawfully and required him to appear in the lineup, with others, conducted without notice to his attorney. He was identified in court at his trial by witnesses who had also identified him at the lineup.

In Stovall, the accused was identified by the victim from her hospital bed, two days after an assault in which her husband had been killed. Her condition was such (she had been stabbed 11 times in the assault) that it was doubtful if she would live. In this case Stovall was not in any lineup. He was the only person brought before the identifying witness, - a "one-to-one" confrontation. The victim survived and identified him at the trial. Stovall had no attorney at his identification in the hospital. At the confrontation with the victim he was required to speak some words for voice identification.

In all three cases the petitioners had been convicted. In Wade and Gilbert the lineups were conducted after indictment and after they had counsel. In Stovall an arraignment was promptly held but was postponed until he could retain counsel.

All three petitioners argued that their constitutional rights under the Fifth, Sixth and Fourteenth (Due Process Clause) Amendments were violated. These contentions were disposed of as follows:

B. THE LAW AND ANALYSIS OF THE AUTHORITIES.

    1. FIFTH AMENDMENT CLAIM (SELF-INCRIMINATION). There is no violation of the Fifth Amendment in compelling an accused to appear in a lineup to

exhibit his features to a prosecution witness; or to repeat words for voice identification; or to give handwriting examplars. These acts do not constitute testimonial compulsion. (Schmerber v. California, 384US75; Holt v. United States, 218US245).

In this connection, Mr. Justice Brennan, speaking for the majority of the court said:

> "We have no doubt that compelling the accused merely to exhibit his person for observation by a prosecution witness prior to trial involves no compulsion of the accused to give evidence having testimonial significance. It is compulsion of the accused to exhibit his physical characteristics, not compulsion to disclose any knowledge he might have . . . Similarly, compelling Wade to speak within hearing distance of the witnesses, even to utter words purportedly uttered by the robber, was not compulsion to utter statements of a 'testimonial' nature; he was required to use his voice as an identifying physical characteristic, not to speak his guilt . . . The distinction to be drawn under the Fifth Amendment privilege against self-incrimination is one between an accused's 'communications' in whatever form, vocal or physical, and 'compulsion which makes a suspect or accused the source of real or physical evidence' . . . (the privilege) offers no protection against compulsion to submit to fingerprinting, photography or measurements, to write or speak for identification, to appear in court, to stand, to assume a stance, to walk, or to make a particular gesture . . . None of these activities become testimonial within the scope of the privilege because required of the accused in a pretrial lineup." (Wade, supra).

In Holt, supra, the accused prior to trial, and over his protest, was required to don certain clothing that fitted him, for the purpose of identification. This act, the Court held, did not violate his Fifth Amendment privilege. The prohibition of the Fifth Amendment against compelling a man to give evidence against himself is a prohibition of the use of physical or moral compulsion to <u>extort communications</u> from him and not an exclusion of his body as evidence when it is material.

> "Another objection is based upon an extravagant extension of the Fifth Amendment. A question arose as to whether a blouse belonged to the prisoner. A witness testified that the prisoner put it on and it fitted him. It is objected that he did this under the same duress that made his statements inadmissible, and that it should be excluded for the same reasons. But the prohibition of compelling a man in a criminal court to be a witness against himself is a prohibition of the use of physical or moral compulsion to extort communications from him, not an exclusion of his body as evidence when it may be material. The objection in principle would forbid a jury to look at a prisoner and compare his features with a photograph in proof. Moreover, we need not consider how far a court would go in compelling a man to exhibit himself. For when he is exhibited whether voluntarily or by order, and even if the order goes too far, the evidence, if material is competent. <u>Adams v. New York</u>, 192US585." (<u>Holt</u>, supra, pp. 252,253).

It is to be noted that the judicial history of the Fifth Amendment privilege has always indicated that the privilege is to be interpreted as applying to testimonial compulsion, i.e., compelling persons to speak and thus incriminate themselves by uttering words or producing records (<u>Boyd v. United States</u>, 116US616).

<u>Wigmore</u> has stated the rule to the same effect. It is no more logical, he writes, for a defendant to

The Law

refuse to go into a courtroom for trial on the ground that by exposing his features in the courtroom to the witnesses for identification was in violation of his privilege against self-incrimination than to compel an accused to submit to an examination of his body features. Obviously, he says, there must be a limit to the privilege.

> "That he (the accused) may in such cases be required sometimes to exercise muscular action – as when he is required to take off his shoes or roll up his sleeve – is immaterial, unless all bodily action were synonomous with testimonial utterance; for, as already observed (secs. 2263, supra), not compulsion alone is the component idea of the privilege, but testimonial compulsion. What is obtained from the accused by such action is not testimony about his body, but his body itself . . . When the person's body, its marks and traits, itself is in issue, there is ordinarily no other or better evidence available for the prosecutor. Hence, the public interest in obtaining the evidence is usually sufficient to outweigh by a clear margin the private interests sacrificed in the process." (8Wigmore on Evidence, sec. 2265, p. 386).

Wigmore then lists a variety of acts which have been ruled upon as not covered by the Fifth Amendment privilege:

a. Routine fingerprinting, photographing or measuring of a suspect.

b. imprinting of portions of a suspect's body (e.g., foot in mud, nose and cheek on window) for purposes of identification.

c. examination of the body of a suspect for identifying characteristics.

d. examination of the body of a suspect, including

his private parts, for evidence of disease or crime.

e. extraction of substance from inside the body of suspect for purposes of analysis and use in evidence (see blood tests, supra).

f. removing from or placing on a suspect, shoes or head coverings or other clothing (see Holt, supra).

g. requiring a suspect to speak for identification (see Wade, Gilbert, Stovall).

h. requiring a suspect to write for identification.

i. requiring a suspect to appear in court, stand, assume a stance, walk or make a particular gesture.

j. requiring a suspect to submit to an examination for sanity (Wigmore, ibid., pp.387-399).

The rule is traced back to Lilburn (1637)(3How.St. Tr.1315,1321), a case that was initiated in the notorious courts of Star Chamber and of High Commission. These courts were abolished in 1641 and with them was swept away the "ex officio" oath required of a suspect to answer criminal charges, under oath, as to matters under investigation before those courts, in the absence of a charge or presentment having been filed against the suspect.

The right of an individual not to incriminate himself on any charge, in any court, civil or ecclesiastical, was first raised in 1649 in the case of the Twelve Bishops (4How.State Trials993,1101). The claim was subsequently upheld in The Protector v. Lord Lumley Hardres, in 1655. By 1700 the practice of questioning the accused had disappeared (Wigmore, ibid., sec.2250, p.289 et seq.;

Sir James Stephen, I Hist. Crim. Law 440).

"**Historically,** the privilege against self-incrimination **originated** as a reaction to the practice in **the early English** courts of compelling a witness to be sworn **and give testimony** concerning his guilt or innocence." (State v. King, 209A(2)110; 8Wigmore on Evidence (McNaughton Rev. 1961) sec.2250).

Strangely **enough the doctrine** of "self-incrimination" was **ignored in the** Colonies. Agitation for its inclusion in our Bill of Rights did not make itself evident until the French Revolution, when the Third Estate (France) voted to abolish compulsory sworn interrogations of the accused in 1789. Such inquisitorial interrogations were authorized in France by the Ordonnance of 1670 (Wigmore, ibid., p. 293).

2. SIXTH AMENDMENT CLAIM - RIGHT TO COUNSEL " CRITICAL STAGE". This Amendment provides, as applicable here, that "In all criminal prosecutions the accused shall . . . have the Assistance of Counsel for his defense." This right to counsel has been interpreted to apply to every "critical stage" of a criminal proceeding. The term "critical stage" is defined as that stage of a criminal proceeding where rights are preserved or irretrievably lost. (White v. Maryland, 373US59; Hamilton v. Alabama, 368US52,53,54; Powell v. Alabama, 287US45, 69; People v. Sykes, 23AD(2)701, 258NYS (2)275). In Alabama, for example, rights not asserted at an arraignment, may not be retrieved.

In Hamilton, ibid., the Court referred to this fact in stating "What happens there, (at the arraignment) may affect the whole trial. Available defenses may be irretrievably lost, if not then and there asserted."

3. EXAMPLES OF "CRITICAL STAGE" WHERE COUNSEL IS REQUIRED. Other examples of "critical stage" of the proceeding (the right to the aid and assistance of counsel) are:

a. during an in-custodial interrogation (Miranda v. Arizona, supra, 384US436; Escobedo v. Illinois, supra, 378US478).

b. after a defendant has been arrested, indicted, informed against by a Grand Jury (information or presentment) or after the commencement of judicial proceedings against him (Miranda, ibid; Escobedo, ibid; Massiah v. United States, 377 US201; People v. Witenski, 15NY(2)392; People v Donovan, 13NY(2)148).

c. at the time of sentencing (Carter v. Illinois, 329US173,178; Powell v. Alabama, supra; Hamilton v. Alabama, supra).

d. in certain jurisdictions, depending on local law, the time of arraignment (United States v. Pointer, 380US400, White v. Maryland, supra; Hamilton v. Alabama, supra; United States v. Reincke, 333F(2)608).

e. a change of plea to guilty, offered during trial, even though the defendant had been defending himself pro se (Davis v. Holman , 354F(2)773; Matter of DeToro, 222F.Supp.621; People v. Thompson, 26AD(2)938).

f. on a charge of violation of probation (Mempa

v. Rhay, 389US128; <u>People v. Reynolds</u>, 25AD(2) 487; <u>People v. Hamilton</u>, 26AD(2)134).

g. in habeas corpus sanity hearings (<u>People ex rel Stanley v. Rogers</u>, 17NY(2)256; <u>People ex rel Rodriguez v. LaValee</u>, 26AD(2)8).

h. in a coram nobis hearing (<u>People v. Monahan</u>, 17NY(2)310).

i. in a courts martial (<u>Application of Stapely</u>, 246F.Supp.316; <u>United States v. Tempia</u>, (U.S. Court of Military Appeals), 35L.W.2625; <u>People v. Benjamin</u>, 28AD(2)106, 281NYS(2)405).

The reason for the rule is logical. It is that "the accused is guaranteed that he need not stand alone against the State at any stage of the prosecution, formal or informal, in the court or out, where counsel's absence might derogate the accused's right to a fair trial." (Mr. J. Brennan, supra).

Differentiating between situations where the accused is not entitled to the presence of counsel, such as at the time of taking of fingerprints, or a sample of blood, hair or clothing, (<u>Schmerber v. California</u>, supra; <u>Holt v. United States</u>, supra), (see also discussion under Fifth Amendment, supra), and lineup identification, he pointed out that the latter situation contained many dangers and factors which might seriously impair a fair trial. Some of these factors is the danger of an unfair lineup, in which the accused is pinpointed as the culprit- also the "rigged" lineup, conscious or unconscious.

"Thus in the present context, where so many variables and pitfalls exist, the first line of defense must be the prevention of unfairness and the lessening of the hazards of eyewitness identification at the line-up itself . . .

"Since it appears that there is a grave potential for prejudice, intentional or not, in the pretrial line-up, which may not be capable of reconstruction at trial, and since presence of counsel itself can often avert prejudice and assure meaningful confrontation at trial, there can be little doubt that for Wade the post-indictment line-up was a critical stage of the prosecution at which he was 'as much entitled to such aid (of counsel) . . . as at the trial itself. Thus, both Wade and his counsel should have been notified of the impending line-up, and counsel's presence should have been a requisite to conduct of the line-up, absent an "intelligent waiver." ' "

The majority of the Court thus concluded that a pre-trial identification lineup is a "critical stage" of a criminal proceeding at which an accused was entitled to the aid and presence of counsel.

"Identification of the suspect - a prerequisite to establishment of guilt - occurs at this stage . . ." (Pointer v. Texas, 380US400).

4. WAIVER OF RIGHT TO COUNSEL. If presence of counsel is waived, it must be an "Intelligent waiver" (Carnley v. Cochran, 369US506).

5. EFFECT OF VIOLATION OF RIGHT TO COUNSEL ON IN-COURT IDENTIFICATION - HARMLESS ERROR RULE. The fact that an accused's rights to counsel at the lineup identification was violated does not make his in-court identification by the same lineup witness excludable for that reason. "A per se exclusion would be unthinkable."

However, if the lineup identification was based on evidence unlawfully seized from the accused (i.e., in violation of the Fourth Amendment), the in-court identification is excludable per se,

When, however, the lineup identification was conducted in the absence of or notice to counsel (absent a waiver), the People must be given an opportunity at "a hearing to determine whether the in-court identifications had an independent source," or whether they were the tainted fruits of the unlawfully conducted lineup or were mere harmless error (Chapman v. California, 386US18; Wong Sun v. United States, 371US471; People v. Ballot, 20NY (2)600; People v. Brown, 20NY(2)238; see also NY C.C.P., sec.542).

a. The Hearing. The People have the burden of establishing at such a hearing the contention of "non-taint" or "harmless error" by "clear and convincing" evidence.

The hearing should take place in the absence of the jury, and, absent legislation or guidelines laid down by some appropriate court, the hearing will undoubtedly follow the procedures used in suppressal and Huntley hearings. (Mapp v. Ohio, 367US643; People v. Huntley, 15NY(2)72; People v. Huntley (Huntley Guidelines), 46Misc (2)209; People v. Wright, 277NYS(2)695; People v. Brown, NYLJ, 8/28/67 p.17/7; People v. Smiley, 284NYS(2)265) (see also proposed N.Y. C.C.P. Art.375).

The District Court of Nassau County in New York has held that identification of a defendant should not be ordered suppressed in advance of trial, but such determination should be made by the trial judge, in the absence of the jury, depending on how the evidence is presented. "The position of the Supreme Court in Wade (supra) is far from clear . * * * There is also a major public policy determination as to the desirability of compelling witnesses to make so many trips to court that the prosecution expires from exhaustion prior to actual trial." (People v. Bianco, 55Misc(2)903).

b. Tainted In-Court Identification - Wong Sun. In Wade, the police seized a photograph of the petitioner from his apartment, in violation of his Fourth Amendment rights. That photograph was shown to a witness who thereafter identified him in the lineup. The Court in this instance applied the rule laid down in Wong Sun, supra, which is "whether, granting establishment of the primary illegality, the evidence to which instant objection is made has been come at by exploitation of the illegality or instead by means sufficiently distinguishable to be purged of the primary taint."

In Simmons v. United States (US , dec. 3/18/68) there had been a pre-trial identification by eye witnesses who were shown several photographs the day after the robbery. Each witness, while alone, was shown the pictures and asked to identify the robbers. The court stated, that although this was not an ideal procedure, there was nothing in the photographic identification that was ". . . so impermissibly suggestive as to give rise to a very substantial likelihood of irreparable misidentification," particularly when made only a day after the crime while "memories are still fresh."

c. Test for Harmless Error - Wong Sun Rule. Under this test, the cases of Wade, Gilbert and Stovall require an examination of the following factors:

(1) prior opportunity to observe the alleged criminal act,

(2) the existence of any discrepancy between lineup description and the defendant's actual appearance,

(3) any identification prior to lineup of another person as the culprit,

(4) any identification of the defendant by picture prior to the lineup,

(5) any failure by the identifier to identify the defendant on a prior occasion,

(6) the lapse of time between the commission of the alleged criminal act and the lineup identification.

d. Additional Areas of Examination are:

(1) how was the lineup actually conducted - the physical arrangements of the suspect with others, if any; clothing worn by those in the lineup, etc.

(2) was there any prior relationship between the accused and the suspect; were they strangers to each other, friends, relatives or

acquaintances,

(3) how long were they together during the commission of the alleged crime. (<u>People v. Brown</u>, supra; <u>People v. Ballot</u>, supra.)

6. <u>"TAINTED" IN-COURT IDENTIFICATION - EX-CEPTION</u>. However, courtroom identification is not barred "where there has been no previous identification in the presence of the police although the defendant is known to be in custody and charged with the commission of a crime." This is the rule even though the courtroom witness sees the accused handcuffed in the courtroom or otherwise observes that he is the defendant in the very case in which he will be called upon to identify the defendant as the culprit.

Such a situation, it would seem presents ample ground for attempting to impeach the witness' identification testimony on the ground that it is highly suggestive and leading and constitutes, in effect, a face-to-face confrontation - a practice generally condemned by the courts. See <u>Stovall</u>, infra; and <u>Palmer v. Peyton</u>, 359 F(2)199.

7. <u>THE FOURTEENTH AMENDMENT AND DUE PROCESS CLAIM</u>. As a result of the decision in <u>Gideon v. Wainwright</u> (372US335), which overruled <u>Betts v. Brady</u> (316US455), the United States Supreme Court has absorbed the Sixth Amendment right to the assistance of counsel into the Due Process clause of the Fourteenth Amendment com-

pletely. This rule has not yet been applied to all pre-trial investigatory procedures, although in Wade, Gilbert and Stovall it is now the rule that it is applicable to pre-trial lineup identifications held after June 12, 1967. (See Retroactivity, infra.)

If the lineup identification is removed from the "critical stage" of the proceedings by appropriate legislation or police department regulations (infra), then the right to counsel at the lineup would be eliminated.

Nevertheless, and in spite of the fact that a defendant does not have available to himself the right to counsel claim at the lineup identification at which he had no counsel present, he may still attack the lineup identification on the ground that it was made under circumstances that were so unfair as to constitute a denial of "due process of law" guaranteed by the Fourteenth Amendment, e.g., that it was conducted in a manner so unnecessarily suggestive that it was conducive to irreparable mistaken identification (Palmer v. Peyton, supra, 359 F(2)199).

The practice of showing a suspect singly, and not as part of a lineup, has been widely condemned and may constitute an important element of unfiarness.

The "Totality of Circumstances" Exception
However, such single, one-to-one confrontation is not, ipso facto, unfair. It must be adjudged and considered in the "totality of the circumstances" present. Such a "totality of circumstances" in Stovall

requires the conclusion that the "single showing" was "imperative." (See <u>Stovall</u> facts, supra.) it was imperative, among other reasons, because it was doubtful if the identifying witness (the only surviving victim of the crime), would live. A situation, very similar to a dying declaration, seems to have been present. Additionally the court pointed out, she was the only person who could exonerate the defendant Stovall.

Under such a "totality of circumstances" making a "single showing" of the accused imperative, there was no violation of the due process clause of the Fourteenth Amendment. Accordingly, no hearing as to the lineup identification is required in this type of situation. (Cf., <u>People v. Ballot</u>, (supra, 20NY(2) 600,607) in which the court said, "We cannot say, as we could in <u>Brown</u> (<u>People v. Brown</u>, supra, 20 NY(2)238) that on the record before us the in-court identification was not predicated, at least in part, upon the earlier grossly and unnecessarily suggestive show-up in the police station a year after the crime had been committed." ". . . there must be a new trial . . . And, upon the retrial, the People may introduce Mrs. Seidman's in-court identification only if they establish, by clear and convincing proof, at a hearing to be held by the judge out of the presence of the jury, that it is based upon observations of the subject other than the police station identification."

In a somewhat parallel case the United States Supreme Court affirmed a conviction for rape, without opinion, where the confrontation of the victim and the defendant took place in a police station seven months after the crime. In effect this affirmation held that such confrontation, after the lapse of seven months, was not so unduly unfair as to taint defendant's conviction for rape.

It must be noted that this affirmance was by an equally divided court. The dissenting opinion by Mr. Justice Douglas, in which 3 other Justices joined, may be of great value as a guideline in resolving issues concerning identification procedures followed by the police.

The Dissenting Opinion

Seven months after she had been raped in January 1965 the complainant was brought to the station house to, as she was told, "look at a suspect." Complainant was only able to identify defendant, as he stood alone in a doorway, by the sound of his voice when he was required to repeat the words spoken by the rapist. Five policemen were present to observe this confrontation but neither the parents of defendant (he was 16 years old) nor an attorney acting for him were notified.

While observing that "due process is not always violated when the police fail to assemble a lineup but conduct a one-man showup," the Court held that in view of the totality of surrounding circumstances the procedure followed here was unnecessarily suggestive and impermissible. Complainant was informed she was going to view a "suspect" seven

months after the rape which had occurred in an
open area by moonlight. Her identification rested
mainly upon his voice without relating any pecu-
liarities of his speech. Moreover, she did not
identify him in the courtroom. It was held the entire
atmosphere of police surrounding complainant in the
precinct as they showed a suspect singly was "preg-
nant with prejudice" and so powerfully suggestive
that her identification constituted a violation of due
process. Defendant is entitled to a new trial un-
affected by the station house identification and the
testimony of officers who were present when it took
place. (Biggers v. Tennessee,   US   (dec.3/18/68).

8. RETROACTIVITY OF WADE-GILBERT-STOVALL

The cut-off date for the applicability of the Wade-
Gilbert decisions is June 12,1967. Those decisions
affect only Wade and Gilbert "and all future cases
which involve confrontations for identification purposes conducted in the absence of counsel." (i.e.
cases after June 12, 1967).

This new rule also excludes Stovall and additionally it excludes as well "convictions at various
stages of trial and direct review." This means that
the Wade-Gilbert rules do not apply to cases still
in the trial stage or in the stream of direct appellate review. Wade and Gilbert alone are the "chance
beneficiaries" of the new rule, even though there
are other litigants who have raised the same
issues. (Johnson v. New Jersey, 384US719, 725-727;
Linkletter v. Walker, 381US618; Tehan v. Shott,

382US406; cf. <u>Mapp v. Ohio</u>, 367US643; <u>Miranda</u> <u>v. Arizona</u>, 384US436).

9. ELIMINATING THE "CRITICAL STAGE OF THE PROCEEDINGS" FROM LINEUP IDENTIFICATIONS

In spite of its ruling that pre-trial identification of a defendant is a "critical stage" of a criminal proceeding requiring "the guiding hand of counsel," the Court nevertheless held that certain action could be taken by legislation or appropriate police department regulations to remove the "critical stage" connotation.

"Legislative or other regulations, such as those of local police departments, which eliminate the risks of abuse and unintentional suggestion at line-up proceedings and the impediments to meaningful confrontation at trial may also remove the basis for regarding the stage as 'critical.' "

Such a police department regulation has been issued by the New York City Police Department (T.O.P. #318) and has been set forth in full in Appendix A.

10. SUMMARY OF WADE-GILBERT-STOVALL.

a. An accused may be required to appear in a lineup for identification purposes.

b. The lineup is a critical stage of a criminal proceeding.

c. He is entitled to the right of counsel at the lineup and must be so advised.

d. He may waive his right to counsel, providing

it is an intelligent waiver.

e. Appropriate legislation or meaningful police department regulations may remove the lineup identification from the "critical stage" connotation and the concomitant right to counsel.

f. These new strictures apply only to those cases occuring after June 12, 1967. They are not retroactive and are not applicable to cases on trial, where the trial commenced before June 12, 1967, or to cases in the normal stream of direct appellate review.

g. Failure to notify the defendant of his right to counsel at the lineup (absent an "intelligent waiver") does not render his identification, at the trial itself, by the witness who identified him at the lineup (in-court identification) per se excludable.

(1) If the lineup identification was made after the identifying witness had been shown a photograph of the defendant which had been unlawfully seized from his apartment by virtue of an unlawful search and seizure, the in-court identification is per se excludable.

(2) Granting a violation of the defendant's Sixth Amendment rights, the People are entitled to a hearing to determine whether the in-court identification had an independent source, or was the tainted fruits of an unlawfully conducted lineup.

(3) The hearing should be conducted by the court in the absence of the jury.

(4) The burden is on the People to establish "non-taint" by clear and convincing evidence.

h. If the hearing discloses "no taint" or that the lineup identification constituted mere harmless error, the in-court identification is admissible.

i. The fact that the defendant appears in the courtroom handcuffed, in custody of the police or as otherwise pin-pointed as the defendant, does not render his in-court identification excludable.

j. Showing a suspect singly in a "one-to-one lineup" to an identifying witness, pre-trial is condemned. However, in certain cases, depending on the "totality of the circumstances" rendering such direct confrontation "imperative," there is no unfairness or violation of the Due Process clause of the Fourteenth Amendment in such single confrontation.

k. Even though a defendant may not be permitted to avail himself of the Wade-Gilbert rulings (see Retroactivity, supra), nevertheless he may attack his lineup identification if it was conducted under circumstances so unfair as to constitute a denial of Due Process under the Fourteenth Amendment.

l. Requiring a defendant, prior to trial, to exhibit his body, to don certain clothing similar to that of the alleged assailant, requiring him to repeat certain words for voice identification, or assume a stance, make a gesture, wear certain items on his face, or the taking of samples of his blood, clothing, hair, handwriting exemplars, and the like, does not constitute testimonial compulsion in violation of a defendant's rights against self-incrimination under the Fifth Amendment.

m. Although <u>Wade-Gilbert</u> and <u>Stovall</u> are post-indictment cases, they undoubtedly apply to pre-indictment cases also.

11. ACTION OF COUNSEL AT THE LINEUP. How far may counsel interject himself in the lineup proceedings? May he advise his client not to participate, or to participate only under certain circumstances and conditions? These questions were raised by Mr. Justice Clark in his dissent (18L. Ed.(2)1168). What is the remedy if the attorney's acts are primarily obstructional? (Yale Law Journal Vol. 77, pp. 390,396(1967)).

Other questions present themselves.

Assuming that the physical arrangement of the lineup identification procedure is suggestive and unfair, and counsel, being present, does nothing to correct it. Such inaction of counsel could militate against the defendant at the hearing if defendant urged an "unfair lineup and tainted in-court identification. The prosecutor could ask defendant. 'You say the lineup was unfair - but your attorney was present. He did nothing about it.' "

If the defendant physically resisted going into the lineup, would this not pinpoint him and result in his identification, inspired in part by his own acts?

These opinions raise many questions which are still to be resolved.

APPENDIX A

POLICE   DEPARTMENT   T.O.P. 318
CITY OF NEW YORK

July 26, 1967

TO ALL COMMANDS:

Subject: POLICE "LINE-UP" FOR IDENTIFICATION.

1.   On June 12, 1967, the United States Supreme Court in three cases indicated that certain procedural safeguards must be established before law enforcement officers submit a person in custody to a "line-up" at the station house or other place of confinement for the purposes of identification by the victim of or the witness to a crime. If these certain safeguards are not followed the identifying witness may be precluded from making a subsequent court room identification of the suspect.

2.   Therefore, in order to assure a fair proceeding, the following rules must be followed whenever a person in police custody is to be viewed in a "line-up" by the victims of a crime, witnesses or other persons for the purpose of establishing the suspect's identity or connection with the crime:

a.   The subject shall be advised that he is going to be viewed by others for the purpose of establishing his identity insofar as a particular crime or crimes are concerned, and he shall also be advised that he is entitled to have an attorney present during such proceeding, if the attorney may be made available without undue delay. If the subject requests that an attorney be notified to be present during such "line-up," the member of the force conducting the investigation shall make every reasonable effort to contact the attorney selected and advise him that he may be present during a "line-up" at a certain time and place. After a reasonable time, if the attorney does not appear, the "line-up" may begin.

b.   The officer conducting the investigation shall give the attorney for the subject a reasonable opportunity to attend the "line-up," consistent with the prevailing circumstances such as the hour of the day or night, the condition of the victim or witnesses involved and any other pertinent circumstances.

c.   The subject may also be advised that the presence of an attorney may be waived. In these cases, the subject's consent to be viewed without an attorney present must be expressly given and must be free from any threats, inducements or promises.

d.   If an attorney for the subject is present during the "line-up," he shall be permitted to observe the manner in which the "line-up" is conducted. He shall not be permitted to talk to any of the witnesses participating in the identification of the subject. Any suggestion that the attorney may make concerning the conduct of the "line-up" to improve the fairness of the procedure shall be followed by the officer conducting the "line-up," if, in the officer's judgment, the suggestions are reasonable and practical.

e.   All "line-ups" conducted in the station house or other place of custody by members of this department shall be conducted in the following manner:

(1)   The defendant or suspect should be viewed with at least four (4) other persons of the same sex, race and approximately the same age, height, weight and manner of dress. The subject shall be permitted to select his position in the group and he may change his position if he so desires at any time during the course of the "line-up."

(2)   There must be no visible indication as to which of the group is in custody for the particular offense.

(3)   No member of the group may be asked to say or do anything to facilitate identification unless all are asked to do the same thing.

T.O.P. 318

(4)   No interrogation of any member of the group may occur in the presence of the viewing witness or victim.

(5)   Special care must be taken that no member of the group be seen by the witness or victim prior to his appearance in the group.

(6)   Two (2) or more victims or witnesses should not view the same suspect or defendant in each other's presence nor should they be permitted to communicate with each other during the viewing procedure. The fact that one or more of them may have made a positive or negative identification may not be revealed to the others. The witnesses or victim may remain unseen or masked when viewing the "line-up."

(7)   If practicable, a photograph should be taken of the entire group, including the suspect or defendant, viewed by the identifying witness or victim showing their physical appearance at the time and the clothing worn for purposes of the identification.

(8)   The police officer or other official conducting the viewing shall record fully, on U.F. 61, D.D. 5 or U.F. 49, as appropriate, the details of the procedure utilized including specific utterances and actions required of the group to facilitate identification, all of the responses of the viewing witness or victim, and the time intervals involved. The names and addresses of all participants in the viewing must also be recorded. This includes, in addition to the suspect or defendant and the victim or other witnesses, the others in the group with the suspect or defendant; the police officers or other officials present; any lawyer, friend or relative of any suspect or defendant; any other persons participating in or witnessing the conduct of the viewing procedure.

(9)   No person present at such viewing or any person participating therein shall do any act or say anything calculated to or likely to influence the identifying witness or victim to make or not to make a particular identification. Specifically, no suggestions, direct or indirect, may be communicated to the witness or victim as to which member of the group is believed to be the culprit or non-culprit. Nothing may be said to or in the presence of the witness or victim which suggests, in any way, which member or whether any member of the group has been arrested for the offense in question or for any other offence. Personal details relating to any member of the group may not be revealed. A positive or negative identification, if any, must in all cases be the product of the free choice of the identifying witness or victim, as based wholly upon independent recollection and recognition. It is the responsibility of the officer conducting the proceeding to take all appropriate precautions to this end.

f.   In the cases where it may be necessary to have the victim or of or the witness to a crime identify the subject at a place other than a station house or other place of detention, such as a hospital, because the victim or witness is seriously incapacitated, or because the victim or witness is in critical condition and the identification cannot be delayed because of the possibility of impending death, and the provisions of the preceding instructions cannot be fully complied with, the officer conducting the investigation may conduct the identification process in whatever manner possible, consistent with the requirements of fairness.

g.   Any interrogation of the suspect or defendant, whether it precedes or follows the "line-up," must be in accordance with the provisions of T.O.P. 224, s. 1966.

3.   Commanding officers and supervisory heads shall be responsible that members of their commands are instructed in and comply with the provisions of this order.

BY DIRECTION OF THE POLICE COMMISSIONER.

SANFORD D. GARELIK,
Chief Inspector

LB/m2
Distribution:
  To all commands

INACTIVE DATE: Upon issuance of   - 2 -   T.O.P. 318
               subsequent orders.

114

APPENDIX B

UNITED STATES *v.* WADE.

No. 334.   Argued February 16, 1967.—Decided June 12, 1967.

Several weeks after respondent's indictment for robbery of a federally insured bank and for conspiracy, respondent, without notice
to his appointed counsel, was placed in a lineup in which each
person wore strips of tape on his face, as the robber allegedly had
done, and on direction repeated words like those the robber
allegedly had used.   Two bank employees identified respondent
as the robber.   At the trial when asked if the robber was in the
courtroom, they identified respondent.   The prior lineup identifications were elicited on cross-examination.   Urging that the conduct of the lineup violated his Fifth Amendment privilege against
self-incrimination and his Sixth Amendment right to counsel,
respondent filed a motion for judgment of acquittal or, alternatively, to strike the courtroom identifications.   The trial court
denied the motions and respondent was convicted.   The Court of
Appeals reversed, holding that though there was no Fifth Amendment deprivation the absence of counsel at the lineup denied
respondent his right to counsel under the Sixth Amendment and
required the grant of a new trial at which the in-court identifications of those who had made lineup identifications would be
excluded.   *Held:*

1. Neither the lineup itself nor anything required therein violated
respondent's Fifth Amendment privilege against self-incrimination
since merely exhibiting his person for observation by witnesses
and using his voice as an identifying physical characteristic involved no compulsion of the accused to give evidence of a testimonial nature against himself which is prohibited by that
Amendment.   Pp. 221–223.

2. The Sixth Amendment guarantees an accused the right to
counsel not only at his trial but at any critical confrontation by
the prosecution at pretrial proceedings where the results might
well determine his fate and where the absence of counsel might
derogate from his right to a fair trial.   Pp. 223–227.

3. The post-indictment lineup (unlike such preparatory steps
as analyzing fingerprints and blood samples) was a critical prose-
cutive stage at which respondent was entitled to the aid of counsel.
Pp. 227–239.

UNITED STATES v. WADE.

(a) There is a great possibility of unfairness to the accused at that point, (1) because of the manner in which confrontations for identification are frequently conducted, (2) because of dangers inherent in eyewitness identification and suggestibility inherent in the context of the confrontations, and (3) because of the likelihood that the accused will often be precluded from reconstructing what occurred and thereby obtaining a full hearing on the identification issue at trial. Pp. 229–235.

(b) This case illustrates the potential for improper influence on witnesses through the lineup procedure, since the bank employees were allowed to see respondent in the custody of FBI agents before the lineup began. Pp. 233–234.

(c) The presence of counsel at the lineup will significantly promote fairness at the confrontation and a full hearing at trial on the issue of identification. Pp. 236–238.

4. In-court identification by a witness to whom the accused was exhibited before trial in the absence of counsel must be excluded unless it can be established that such evidence had an independent origin or that error in its admission was harmless. Since it is not clear that the Court of Appeals applied the prescribed rule of exclusion, and since the nature of the in-court identifications here was not an issue in the trial and cannot be determined on the record, the case must be remanded to the District Court for resolution of these issues. Pp. 239–243.

358 F. 2d 557, vacated and remanded.

Beatrice Rosenberg argued the cause for the United States. With her on the brief were *Acting Solicitor General Spritzer, Assistant Attorney General Vinson, Nathan Lewin* and *Ronald L. Gainer.*

Weldon Holcomb argued the cause and filed a brief for respondent.

Mr. Justice Brennan delivered the opinion of the Court.

The question here is whether courtroom identifications of an accused at trial are to be excluded from evidence because the accused was exhibited to the witnesses before trial at a post-indictment lineup conducted for identification purposes without notice to and in the absence of the accused's appointed counsel.

The federally insured bank in Eustace, Texas, was robbed on September 21, 1964. A man with a small strip of tape on each side of his face entered the bank, pointed a pistol at the female cashier and the vice president, the only persons in the bank at the time, and forced them to fill a pillowcase with the bank's money. The man then drove away with an accomplice waiting in a stolen car outside the bank. On March 23, 1965, an indictment was returned against respondent, Wade, and two others for conspiring to rob the bank, and against Wade and the accomplice for the robbery itself. Wade was arrested on April 2, and counsel was appointed to represent him on April 26. Fifteen days later an FBI agent, without notice to Wade's lawyer, arranged to have the two bank employees observe a lineup made up of Wade and five or six other prisoners and conducted in a courtroom of the local county courthouse. Each person in the line wore strips of tape such as allegedly worn by the robber and upon direction each said something like "put the money in the bag," the words allegedly uttered by the robber. Both bank employees identified Wade in the lineup as the bank robber.

At trial, the two employees, when asked on direct examination if the robber was in the courtroom, pointed to Wade. The prior lineup identification was then elicited from both employees on cross-examination. At the close of testimony, Wade's counsel moved for a judgment of acquittal or, alternatively, to strike the bank officials' courtroom identifications on the ground that conduct of the lineup, without notice to and in the absence of his appointed counsel, violated his Fifth Amendment privilege against self-incrimination and his Sixth Amendment right to the assistance of counsel. The motion was denied, and Wade was convicted. The

118

Court of Appeals for the Fifth Circuit reversed the conviction and ordered a new trial at which the in-court identification evidence was to be excluded, holding that, though the lineup did not violate Wade's Fifth Amendment rights, "the lineup, held as it was, in the absence of counsel, already chosen to represent appellant, was a violation of his Sixth Amendment rights . . . ." 358 F. 2d 557, 560. We granted certiorari, 385 U. S. 811, and set the case for oral argument with No. 223, *Gilbert* v. *California, post,* p. 263, and No. 254, *Stovall* v. *Denno, post,* p. 293, which present similar questions. We reverse the judgment of the Court of Appeals and remand to that court with direction to enter a new judgment vacating the conviction and remanding the case to the District Court for further proceedings consistent with this opinion.

I.

Neither the lineup itself nor anything shown by this record that Wade was required to do in the lineup violated his privilege against self-incrimination. We have only recently reaffirmed that the privilege "protects an accused only from being compelled to testify against himself, or otherwise provide the State with evidence of a testimonial or communicative nature . . . ." *Schmerber* v. *California,* 384 U. S. 757, 761. We there held that compelling a suspect to submit to a withdrawal of a sample of his blood for analysis for alcohol content and the admission in evidence of the analysis report was not compulsion to those ends. That holding was supported by the opinion in *Holt* v. *United States,* 218 U. S. 245, in which case a question arose as to whether a blouse belonged to the defendant. A witness testified at trial that the defendant put on the blouse and it had fit him. The defendant argued that the admission of the testimony was error because compelling him to put on the blouse was a violation of his privilege. The Court rejected the claim as "an extravagant extension of the Fifth Amendment," Mr. Justice Holmes saying for the Court:

> "[T]he prohibition of compelling a man in a criminal court to be witness against himself is a prohibition of the use of physical or moral compulsion to extort communications from him, not an exclusion of his body as evidence when it may be material." 218 U. S., at 252–253.

The Court in *Holt,* however, put aside any constitutional questions which might be involved in compelling an accused, as here, to exhibit himself before victims of or witnesses to an alleged crime; the Court stated, "we need not consider how far a court would go in compelling a man to exhibit himself." *Id.,* at 253.[1]

We have no doubt that compelling the accused merely to exhibit his person for observation by a prosecution witness prior to trial involves no compulsion of the accused to give evidence having testimonial significance. It is compulsion of the accused to exhibit his physical characteristics, not compulsion to disclose any knowledge he might have. It is no different from compelling Schmerber to provide a blood sample or Holt to wear the blouse, and, as in those instances, is not within the cover of the privilege. Similarly, compelling Wade to speak within hearing distance of the witnesses, even to utter words purportedly uttered by the robber, was not compulsion to utter statements of a "testimonial" nature; he was required to use his voice as an identifying

---

[1] *Holt* was decided before *Weeks* v. *United States,* 232 U. S. 383, fashioned the rule excluding illegally obtained evidence in a federal prosecution. The Court therefore followed *Adams* v. *New York,* 192 U. S. 585, in holding that, in any event, "when he is exhibited, whether voluntarily or by order, and even if the order goes too far, the evidence, if material, is competent." 218 U. S., at 253.

physical characteristic, not to speak his guilt. We held
in *Schmerber, supra,* at 761, that the distinction to be
drawn under the Fifth Amendment privilege against self-
incrimination is one between an accused's "communications" in whatever form, vocal or physical, and "compulsion which makes a suspect or accused the source of
'real or physical evidence,'" *Schmerber, supra,* at 764.
We recognized that "both federal and state courts have
usually held that . . . [the privilege] offers no protection
against compulsion to submit to fingerprinting, photography, or measurements, to write or speak for identification, to appear in court, to stand, to assume a stance,
to walk, or to make a particular gesture." *Id.,* at 764.
None of these activities becomes testimonial within the
scope of the privilege because required of the accused
in a pretrial lineup.

Moreover, it deserves emphasis that this case presents
no question of the admissibility in evidence of anything
Wade said or did at the lineup which implicates his
privilege. The Government offered no such evidence as
part of its case, and what came out about the lineup
proceedings on Wade's cross-examination of the bank
employees involved no violation of Wade's privilege.

II.

The fact that the lineup involved no violation of
Wade's privilege against self-incrimination does not, however, dispose of his contention that the courtroom identifications should have been excluded because the lineup
was conducted without notice to and in the absence of
his counsel. Our rejection of the right to counsel claim
in *Schmerber* rested on our conclusion in that case that
"[n]o issue of counsel's ability to assist petitioner in respect of any rights he did possess is presented." 384
U. S., at 766. In contrast, in this case it is urged that
the assistance of counsel at the lineup was indispensable

to protect Wade's most basic right as a criminal defendant—his right to a fair trial at which the witnesses against him might be meaningfully cross-examined.

The Framers of the Bill of Rights envisaged a broader role for counsel than under the practice then prevailing in England of merely advising his client in "matters of law," and eschewing any responsibility for "matters of fact." [2] The constitutions in at least 11 of the 13 States expressly or impliedly abolished this distinction. *Powell* v. *Alabama,* 287 U. S. 45, 60–65; Note, 73 Yale L. J. 1000, 1030–1033 (1964). "Though the colonial provisions about counsel were in accord on few things, they agreed on the necessity of abolishing the facts-law distinction; the colonists appreciated that if a defendant were forced to stand alone against the state, his case was foredoomed." 73 Yale L. J., *supra,* at 1033–1034. This background is reflected in the scope given by our decisions to the Sixth Amendment's guarantee to an accused of the assistance of counsel for his defense. When the Bill of Rights was adopted, there were no organized police forces as we know them today.[3] The accused confronted the prosecutor and the witnesses against him, and the evidence was marshalled, largely at the trial itself. In contrast, today's law enforcement machinery involves critical confrontations of the accused by the prosecution at pretrial proceedings where the results might well settle the accused's fate and reduce the trial itself to a mere formality. In recognition of these realities of modern criminal prosecution, our cases have construed the Sixth Amendment guarantee to apply to "critical" stages of the proceedings. The guarantee reads: "In all criminal

[2] See *Powell* v. *Alabama,* 287 U. S. 45, 60–65; Beaney, Right to Counsel in American Courts 8–26.

[3] See Note, 73 Yale L. J. 1000, 1040–1042 (1964); Comment, 53 Calif. L. Rev. 337, 347–348 (1965).

prosecutions, the accused shall enjoy the right . . . to have the Assistance of Counsel *for his defence.*" (Emphasis supplied.) The plain wording of this guarantee thus encompasses counsel's assistance whenever necessary to assure a meaningful "defence."

As early as *Powell* v. *Alabama, supra,* we recognized that the period from arraignment to trial was "perhaps the most critical period of the proceedings . . . ," *id.,* at 57, during which the accused "requires the guiding hand of counsel . . . ," *id.,* at 69, if the guarantee is not to prove an empty right. That principle has since been applied to require the assistance of counsel at the type of arraignment—for example, that provided by Alabama—where certain rights might be sacrificed or lost: "What happens there may affect the whole trial. Available defenses may be irretrievably lost, if not then and there asserted . . . ." *Hamilton* v. *Alabama,* 368 U. S. 52, 54. See *White* v. *Maryland,* 373 U. S. 59. The principle was also applied in *Massiah* v. *United States,* 377 U. S. 201, where we held that incriminating statements of the defendant should have been excluded from evidence when it appeared that they were overheard by federal agents who, without notice to the defendant's lawyer, arranged a meeting between the defendant and an accomplice turned informant. We said, quoting a concurring opinion in *Spano* v. *New York,* 360 U. S. 315, 326, that "[a]nything less . . . might deny a defendant 'effective representation by counsel at the only stage when legal aid and advice would help him.'" 377 U. S., at 204.

In *Escobedo* v. *Illinois,* 378 U. S. 478, we drew upon the rationale of *Hamilton* and *Massiah* in holding that the right to counsel was guaranteed at the point where the accused, prior to arraignment, was subjected to secret interrogation despite repeated requests to see his lawyer. We again noted the necessity of counsel's presence if the accused were to have a fair opportunity to present a defense at the trial itself:

> "The rule sought by the State here, however, would make the trial no more than an appeal from the interrogation; and the 'right to use counsel at the formal trial [would be] a very hollow thing [if], for all practical purposes, the conviction is already assured by pretrial examination'. . . . 'One can imagine a cynical prosecutor saying: "Let them have the most illustrious counsel, now. They can't escape the noose. There is nothing that counsel can do for them at the trial."' " 378 U. S., at 487–488.

Finally in *Miranda* v. *Arizona,* 384 U. S. 436, the rules established for custodial interrogation included the right to the presence of counsel. The result was rested on our finding that this and the other rules were necessary to safeguard the privilege against self-incrimination from being jeopardized by such interrogation.

Of course, nothing decided or said in the opinions in the cited cases links the right to counsel only to protection of Fifth Amendment rights. Rather those decisions "no more than reflect a constitutional principle established as long ago as *Powell* v. *Alabama* . . . ." *Massiah* v. *United States, supra,* at 205. It is central to that principle that in addition to counsel's presence at trial,[4] the accused is guaranteed that he need not stand alone against the State at any stage of the prosecution, formal or informal, in court or out, where counsel's absence might derogate from the accused's right to a fair trial.[5] The security of that right is as much the aim of the right to counsel as it is of the other guarantees of the

---

[4] See, *e. g., Powell* v. *Alabama,* 287 U. S. 45; *Hamilton* v. *Alabama,* 368 U. S. 52; *White* v. *Maryland,* 373 U. S. 59; *Escobedo* v. *Illinois,* 378 U. S. 478; *Massiah* v. *United States,* 377 U. S. 201.

[5] See cases cited n. 4, *supra; Avery* v. *Alabama,* 308 U. S. 444, 446.

Sixth Amendment—the right of the accused to a speedy and public trial by an impartial jury, his right to be informed of the nature and cause of the accusation, and his right to be confronted with the witnesses against him and to have compulsory process for obtaining witnesses in his favor. The presence of counsel at such critical confrontations, as at the trial itself, operates to assure that the accused's interests will be protected consistently with our adversary theory of criminal prosecution. Cf. *Pointer* v. *Texas,* 380 U. S. 400.

In sum, the principle of *Powell* v. *Alabama* and succeeding cases requires that we scrutinize *any* pretrial confrontation of the accused to determine whether the presence of his counsel is necessary to preserve the defendant's basic right to a fair trial as affected by his right meaningfully to cross-examine the witnesses against him and to have effective assistance of counsel at the trial itself. It calls upon us to analyze whether potential substantial prejudice to defendant's rights inheres in the particular confrontation and the ability of counsel to help avoid that prejudice.

III.

The Government characterizes the lineup as a mere preparatory step in the gathering of the prosecution's evidence, not different—for Sixth Amendment purposes—from various other preparatory steps, such as systematized or scientific analyzing of the accused's fingerprints, blood sample, clothing, hair, and the like. We think there are differences which preclude such stages being characterized as critical stages at which the accused has the right to the presence of his counsel. Knowledge of the techniques of science and technology is sufficiently available, and the variables in techniques few enough, that the accused has the opportunity for a meaningful confrontation of the Government's case at trial through the ordinary processes of cross-examination of the Government's expert witnesses and the presentation of the evidence of his own experts. The denial of a right to have his counsel present at such analyses does not therefore violate the Sixth Amendment; they are not critical stages since there is minimal risk that his counsel's absence at such stages might derogate from his right to a fair trial.

IV.

But the confrontation compelled by the State between the accused and the victim or witnesses to a crime to elicit identification evidence is peculiarly riddled with innumerable dangers and variable factors which might seriously, even crucially, derogate from a fair trial. The vagaries of eyewitness identification are well-known; the annals of criminal law are rife with instances of mistaken identification.[6] Mr. Justice Frankfurter once said: "What is the worth of identification testimony even when uncontradicted? The identification of strangers is proverbially untrustworthy. The hazards of such testimony are established by a formidable number of instances in the records of English and American trials. These instances are recent—not due to the brutalities of ancient criminal procedure." The Case of Sacco and Vanzetti 30 (1927). A major factor contributing to the high incidence of miscarriage of justice from mistaken identification has been the degree of suggestion inherent in the manner in which the prosecution presents the suspect to witnesses for pretrial identification. A commenta-

[6] Borchard, Convicting the Innocent; Frank & Frank, Not Guilty; Wall, Eye-Witness Identification in Criminal Cases; 3 Wigmore, Evidence § 786a (3d ed. 1940); Rolph, Personal Identity; Gross, Criminal Investigation 47–54 (Jackson ed. 1962); Williams, Proof of Guilt 83–98 (1955); Wills, Circumstantial Evidence 192–205 (7th ed. 1937); Wigmore, The Science of Judicial Proof §§ 250–253 (3d ed. 1937).

tor has observed that "[t]he influence of improper suggestion upon identifying witnesses probably accounts for
more miscarriages of justice than any other single factor—
perhaps it is responsible for more such errors than all other
factors combined." Wall, Eye-Witness Identification in
Criminal Cases 26. Suggestion can be created intentionally or unintentionally in many subtle ways.[7] And the
dangers for the suspect are particularly grave when the
witness' opportunity for observation was insubstantial,
and thus his susceptibility to suggestion the greatest.

Moreover, "[i]t is a matter of common experience that,
once a witness has picked out the accused at the line-up,
he is not likely to go back on his word later on, so that
in practice the issue of identity may (in the absence of
other relevant evidence) for all practical purposes be
determined there and then, before the trial." [8]

The pretrial confrontation for purpose of identification
may take the form of a lineup, also known as an "identification parade" or "showup," as in the present case, or
presentation of the suspect alone to the witness, as in
Stovall v. *Denno, supra.* It is obvious that risks of suggestion attend either form of confrontation.and increase
the dangers inhering in eyewitness identification.[9] But

---

[7] See Wall, *supra,* n. 6, 26–65; Murray, The Criminal Lineup at
Home and Abroad, 1966 Utah L. Rev. 610; Napley, Problems of
Effecting the Presentation of the Case for a Defendant, 66 Col.
L. Rev. 94, 98–99 (1966); Williams, Identification Parades, [1955]
Crim. L. Rev. (Eng.) 525; Paul, Identification of Accused Persons,
12 Austl. L. J. 42 (1938); Houts, From Evidence to Proof 25;
Williams & Hammelmann, Identification Parades, Parts I & II, [1963]
Crim. L. Rev. 479–490, 545–555; Gorphe, Showing Prisoners to Wit-
nesses for Identification, 1 Am. J. Police Sci. 79 (1930); Wigmore,
The Science of Judicial Proof, *supra,* n. 6, at § 253; Devlin, The
Criminal Prosecution in England 70; Williams, Proof of Guilt 95–97.

[8] Williams & Hammelmann, Identification Parades, Part I, [1963]
Crim. L. Rev. 479, 482.

[9] Williams & Hammelmann, Identification Parades, Part I, *supra,*
n. 7.

as is the case with secret interrogations, there is serious
difficulty in depicting what transpires at lineups and
other forms of identification confrontations. "Privacy
results in secrecy and this in turn results in a gap in
our knowledge as to what in fact goes on . . . ." *Miranda*
v. *Arizona, supra,* at 448. For the same reasons, the
defense can seldom reconstruct the manner and mode of
lineup identification for judge or jury at trial. Those
participating in a lineup with the accused may often be
police officers;[10] in any event, the participants' names
are rarely recorded or divulged at trial.[11] The impediments to an objective observation are increased when the
victim is the witness. Lineups are prevalent in rape and
robbery prosecutions and present a particular hazard
that a victim's understandable outrage may excite venge-
ful or spiteful motives.[12] In any event, neither witnesses
nor lineup participants are apt to be alert for conditions
prejudicial to the suspect. And if they were, it would
likely be of scant benefit to the suspect since neither
witnesses nor lineup participants are likely to be schooled
in the detection of suggestive influences.[13] Improper in-

[10] See Wall, *supra,* n. 6, 57–59; see, *e. g., People* v. *Boney,* 28 Ill.
2d 505, 192 N. E. 2d 920 (1963); *People* v. *James,* 218 Cal. App. 2d
166, 32 Cal. Rptr. 283 (1963).

[11] See Rolph, Personal Identity 50: "The bright burden of identity,
at these parades, is lifted from the innocent participants to hover
about the suspect, leaving the rest featureless and unknown and
without interest."

[12] See Williams & Hammelmann, Identification Parades, Part II,
[1963] Crim. L. Rev. 545, 546; Borchard, Convicting the Innocent
367.

[13] An additional impediment to the detection of such influences
by participants, including the suspect, is the physical conditions
often surrounding the conduct of the lineup. In many, lights shine
on the stage in such a way that the suspect cannot see the witness.
See *Gilbert* v. *United States,* 366 F. 2d 923 (C. A. 9th Cir. 1966).
In some a one-way mirror is used and what is said on the witness'

fluences may go undetected by a suspect, guilty or not, who experiences the emotional tension which we might expect in one being confronted with potential accusers.[14] Even when he does observe abuse, if he has a criminal record he may be reluctant to take the stand and open up the admission of prior convictions. Moreover, any protestations by the suspect of the fairness of the lineup made at trial are likely to be in vain;[15] the jury's choice is between the accused's unsupported version and that of the police officers present.[16] In short, the accused's

side cannot be heard. See *Rigney* v. *Hendrick,* 355 F. 2d 710, 711, n. 2 (C. A. 3d Cir. 1965); *Aaron* v. *State,* 273 Ala. 337, 139 So. 2d 309 (1961).

[14] Williams & Hammelmann, Part I, *supra,* n. 7, at 489; Napley, *supra,* n. 7, at 99.

[15] See *In re Groban,* 352 U. S. 330, 340 (BLACK, J., dissenting). The difficult position of defendants in attempting to protest the manner of pretrial identification is illustrated by the many state court cases in which contentions of blatant abuse rested on their unsupportable allegations, usually controverted by the police officers present. See, *e. g., People* v. *Shields,* 70 Cal. App. 2d 628, 634–635, 161 P. 2d 475, 478–479 (1945); *People* v. *Hicks,* 22 Ill. 2d 364, 176 N. E. 2d 810 (1961); *State* v. *Hill,* 193 Kan. 512, 394 P. 2d 106 (1964); *Redmon* v. *Commonwealth,* 321 S. W. 2d 397 (Ky. Ct. App. 1959); *Lubinski* v. *State,* 180 Md. 1, 8, 22 A. 2d 455, 459 (1941). For a striking case in which hardly anyone agreed upon what occurred at the lineup, including who identified whom, see *Johnson* v. *State,* 237 Md. 283, 206 A. 2d 138 (1965).

[16] An instructive example of the defendant's predicament may be found in *Proctor* v. *State,* 223 Md. 394, 164 A. 2d 708 (1960). A prior identification is admissible in Maryland only under the salutary rule that it cannot have been made "under conditions of unfairness or unreliability." *Id.,* at 401, 164 A. 2d, at 712. Against the defendant's contention that these conditions had not been met, the Court stated:

"In the instant case, there are no such facts as, in our judgment, would call for a finding that the identification . . . was made under conditions of unfairness or unreliability. The relatively large number of persons put into the room together for [the victim] to look at inability effectively to reconstruct at trial any unfairness that occurred at the lineup may deprive him of his only opportunity meaningfully to attack the credibility of the witness' courtroom identification.

What facts have been disclosed in specific cases about the conduct of pretrial confrontations for identification illustrate both the potential for substantial prejudice to the accused at that stage and the need for its revelation at trial. A commentator provides some striking examples:

> "In a Canadian case . . . the defendant had been picked out of a line-up of six men, of which he was the only Oriental. In other cases, a black-haired suspect was placed among a group of light-haired persons, tall suspects have been made to stand with short non-suspects, and, in a case where the perpetrator of the crime was known to be a youth, a suspect under twenty was placed in a line-up with five other persons, all of whom were forty or over " [17]

Similarly state reports, in the course of describing prior identifications admitted as evidence of guilt, reveal

---

is one circumstance indicating fairness, and the fact that the police officer was unable to remember the appearances of the others and could not recall if they had physical characteristics similar to [the defendant's] or not is at least suggestive that they were not of any one type or that they all differed markedly in looks from the defendant. There is no evidence that the Police Sergeant gave the complaining witness any indication as to which of the thirteen men was the defendant; the Sergeant's testimony is simply that he asked [the victim] if he could identify [the defendant] after having put the thirteen men in the courtroom."

[17] Wall, Eye-Witness Identification in Criminal Cases 53. For other such examples see Houts, From Evidence to Proof 25; Frankfurter, The Case of Sacco and Vanzetti 12–14, 30–32; 3 Wigmore, Evidence § 786a, at 164, n. 2 (3d ed. 1940); Paul, Identification of Accused Persons, 12 Austl. L. J. 42, 44 (1938); Rolph, Personal Identity 34–43.

numerous instances of suggestive procedures, for example, that all in the lineup but the suspect were known to the identifying witness,[18] that the other participants in a lineup were grossly dissimilar in appearance from the suspect,[19] that only the suspect was required to wear distinctive clothing which the culprit allegedly wore,[20] that the witness is told by the police that they have caught the culprit after which the defendant is brought before the witness alone or is viewed in jail,[21] that the suspect is pointed out before or during a lineup,[22] and that the participants in the lineup are asked to try on an article of clothing which fits only the suspect.[23]

The potential for improper influence is illustrated by the circumstances, insofar as they appear, surrounding the prior identifications in the three cases we decide today. In the present case, the testimony of the identi-

[18] See *People* v. *James*, 218 Cal. App. 2d 166, 170–171, 32 Cal. Rptr. 283, 286 (1963); *People* v. *Boney*, 28 Ill. 2d 505, 192 N. E. 2d 920 (1963).

[19] See *Fredericksen* v. *United States*, 105 U. S. App. D. C. 262, 266 F. 2d 463 (1959); *People* v. *Adell*, 75 Ill. App. 2d 385, 221 N. E. 2d 72 (1966); *State* v. *Hill*, 193 Kan. 512, 394 P. 2d 106 (1964); *People* v. *Seppi*, 221 N. Y. 62, 116 N. E. 793 (1917); *State* v. *Duggan*, 215 Ore. 151, 162, 333 P. 2d 907, 912 (1958).

[20] See *People* v. *Crenshaw*, 15 Ill. 2d 458, 460, 155 N. E. 2d 599, 602 (1959); *Presley* v. *State*, 224 Md. 550, 168 A. 2d 510 (1961); *State* v. *Ramirez*, 76 N. M. 72, 412 P. 2d 246 (1966); *State* v. *Bazemore*, 193 N. C. 336, 137 S. E. 172 (1927); *Barrett* v. *State*, 190 Tenn. 366, 229 S. W. 2d 516 (1950).

[21] See *Aaron* v. *State*, 273 Ala. 337, 139 So. 2d 309 (1961); *Bishop* v. *State*, 236 Ark. 12, 364 S. W. 2d 676 (1963); *People* v. *Thompson*, 406 Ill. 555, 94 N. E. 2d 349 (1950); *People* v. *Berne*, 384 Ill. 334, 51 N. E. 2d 578 (1943); *People* v. *Martin*, 304 Ill. 494, 136 N. E. 711 (1922); *Barrett* v. *State*, 190 Tenn. 366, 229 S. W. 2d 516 (1950).

[22] See *People* v. *Clark*, 28 Ill. 2d 423, 192 N. E. 2d 851 (1963); *Gillespie* v. *State*, 355 P. 2d 451, 454 (Okla. Cr. 1960).

[23] See *People* v. *Parham*, 60 Cal. 2d 378, 384 P. 2d 1001 (1963).

fying witnesses elicited on cross-examination revealed that those witnesses were taken to the courthouse and seated in the courtroom to await assembly of the lineup. The courtroom faced on a hallway observable to the witnesses through an open door. The cashier testified that she saw Wade "standing in the hall" within sight of an FBI agent. Five or six other prisoners later appeared in the hall. The vice president testified that he saw a person in the hall in the custody of the agent who "resembled the person that we identified as the one that had entered the bank." [24]

The lineup in *Gilbert, supra,* was conducted in an auditorium in which some 100 witnesses to several alleged state and federal robberies charged to Gilbert made wholesale identifications of Gilbert as the robber in each other's presence, a procedure said to be fraught with dangers of suggestion.[25] And the vice of suggestion created by the identification in *Stovall, supra,* was the presentation to the witness of the suspect alone handcuffed to police officers. It is hard to imagine a situation more clearly conveying the suggestion to the witness that the one presented is believed guilty by the police. See Frankfurter, The Case of Sacco and Vanzetti 31–32.

The few cases that have surfaced therefore reveal the existence of a process attended with hazards of serious unfairness to the criminal accused and strongly suggest the plight of the more numerous defendants who are unable to ferret out suggestive influences in the

[24] See Wall, *supra,* n. 6, at 48; Napley, *supra,* n. 7, at 99; "[W]hile many identification parades are conducted by the police with scrupulous regard for fairness, it is not unknown for the identifying witness to be placed in a position where he can see the suspect before the parade forms . . . ."

[25] Williams & Hammelmann, Part I, *supra,* n. 7, at 486; Burtt, Applied Psychology 254–255.

secrecy of the confrontation. We do not assume that these risks are the result of police procedures intentionally designed to prejudice an accused. Rather we assume they derive from the dangers inherent in eyewitness identification and the suggestibility inherent in the context of the pretrial identification. Williams & Hammelmann, in one of the most comprehensive studies of such forms of identification, said, "[T]he fact that the police themselves have, in a given case, little or no doubt that the man put up for identification has committed the offense, and that their chief pre-occupation is with the problem of getting sufficient proof, because he has not 'come clean,' involves a danger that this persuasion may communicate itself even in a doubtful case to the witness in some way . . . ." Identification Parades, Part I, [1963] Crim. L. Rev. 479, 483.

Insofar as the accused's conviction may rest on a courtroom identification in fact the fruit of a suspect pretrial identification which the accused is helpless to subject to effective scrutiny at trial, the accused is deprived of that right of cross-examination which is an essential safeguard to his right to confront the witnesses against him. *Pointer* v. *Texas,* 380 U. S. 400. And even though cross-examination is a precious safeguard to a fair trial, it cannot be viewed as an absolute assurance of accuracy and reliability. Thus in the present context, where so many variables and pitfalls exist, the first line of defense must be the prevention of unfairness and the lessening of the hazards of eyewitness identification at the lineup itself. The trial which might determine the accused's fate may well not be that in the courtroom but that at the pretrial confrontation, with the State aligned against the accused, the witness the sole jury, and the accused unprotected against the overreaching, intentional or unintentional, and with little or no effective appeal from the judgment there rendered by the witness—"that's the man."

Since it appears that there is grave potential for prejudice, intentional or not, in the pretrial lineup, which may not be capable of reconstruction at trial, and since presence of counsel itself can often avert prejudice and assure a meaningful confrontation at trial,[26] there can be

[26] One commentator proposes a model statute providing not only for counsel, but other safeguards as well:

"Most, if not all, of the attacks on the lineup process could be averted by a uniform statute modeled upon the best features of the civilian codes. Any proposed statute should provide for the right to counsel during any lineup or during any confrontation. Provision should be made that any person, whether a victim or a witness, must give a description of the suspect before he views any arrested person. A written record of this description should be required, and the witness should be made to sign it. This written record would be available for inspection by defense counsel for copying before the trial and for use at the trial in testing the accuracy of the identification made during the lineup and during the trial.

"This ideal statute would require at least six persons in addition to the accused in a lineup, and these persons would have to be of approximately the same height, weight, coloration of hair and skin, and bodily types as the suspect. In addition, all of these men should, as nearly as possible, be dressed alike. If distinctive garb was used during the crime, the suspect should not be forced to wear similar clothing in the lineup unless all of the other persons are similarly garbed. A complete written report of the names, addresses, descriptive details of the other persons in the lineup, and of everything which transpired during the identification would be mandatory. This report would include everything stated by the identifying witness during this step, including any reasons given by him as to what features, etc., have sparked his recognition.

"This statute should permit voice identification tests by having each person in the lineup repeat identical innocuous phrases, and it would be impermissible to force the use of words allegedly used during a criminal act.

"The statute would enjoin the police from suggesting to any viewer that one or more persons in the lineup had been arrested as a suspect. If more than one witness is to make an identification, each

little doubt that for Wade the post-indictment lineup was a critical stage of the prosecution at which he was "as much entitled to such aid [of counsel] . . . as at the trial itself." *Powell* v. *Alabama,* 287 U. S. 45, 57. Thus both Wade and his counsel should have been notified of the impending lineup, and counsel's presence should have been a requisite to conduct of the lineup, absent an "intelligent waiver." See *Carnley* v. *Cochran,* 369 U. S. 506. No substantial countervailing policy considerations have been advanced against the requirement of the presence of counsel. Concern is expressed that the requirement will forestall prompt identifications and result in obstruction of the confrontations. As for the first, we note that in the two cases in which the right to counsel is today held to apply, counsel had already been appointed and no argument is made in either case that notice to counsel would have prejudicially delayed the confrontations. Moreover, we leave open the question whether the presence of substitute counsel might not suffice where notification and presence of the suspect's own counsel would result in prejudicial delay.[27] And to refuse to recognize the right to counsel for fear that counsel will obstruct the course of justice is contrary to the

witness should be required to do so separately and should be forbidden to speak to another witness until all of them have completed the process.

"The statute could require the use of movie cameras and tape recorders to record the lineup process in those states which are financially able to afford these devices. Finally, the statute should provide that any evidence obtained as the result of a violation of this statute would be inadmissible." Murray, The Criminal Lineup at Home and Abroad, 1966 Utah L. Rev. 610, 627–628.

[27] Although the right to counsel usually means a right to the suspect's own counsel, provision for substitute counsel may be justified on the ground that the substitute counsel's presence may eliminate the hazards which render the lineup a critical stage for the presence of the suspect's *own* counsel.

basic assumptions upon which this Court has operated
in Sixth Amendment cases. We rejected similar logic
in *Miranda* v. *Arizona* concerning presence of counsel
during custodial interrogation, 384 U. S., at 480–481:

> "[A]n attorney is merely exercising the good pro-
> fessional judgment he has been taught. This is
> not cause for considering the attorney a menace to
> law enforcement. He is merely carrying out what
> he is sworn to do under his oath—to protect to the
> extent of his ability the rights of his client. In ful-
> filling this responsibility the attorney plays a vital
> role in the administration of criminal justice under
> our Constitution."

In our view counsel can hardly impede legitimate law
enforcement; on the contrary, for the reasons expressed,
law enforcement may be assisted by preventing the
infiltration of taint in the prosecution's identification
evidence.[28] That result cannot help the guilty avoid
conviction but can only help assure that the right man
has been brought to justice.[29]

---

[28] Concern is also expressed that the presence of counsel will force
divulgence of the identity of government witnesses whose identity
the Government may want to conceal. To the extent that this is
a valid or significant state interest there are police practices commonly used to effect concealment, for example, masking the face.

[29] Most other nations surround the lineup with safeguards against
prejudice to the suspect. In England the suspect must be allowed
the presence of his solicitor or a friend, Napley, *supra*, n. 7, at
98–99; Germany requires the presence of retained counsel; France
forbids the confrontation of the suspect in the absence of his counsel; Spain, Mexico, and Italy provide detailed procedures prescrib-
ing the conditions under which confrontation must occur under the
supervision of a judicial officer who sees to it that the proceedings
are officially recorded to assure adequate scrutiny at trial. Murray,
The Criminal Lineup at Home and Abroad, 1966 Utah L. Rev.
610, 621–627.

Legislative or other regulations, such as those of local police departments, which eliminate the risks of abuse and unintentional suggestion at lineup proceedings and the impediments to meaningful confrontation at trial may also remove the basis for regarding the stage as "critical." [30]   But neither Congress nor the federal authorities have seen fit to provide a solution. What we hold today "in no way creates a constitutional strait-jacket which will handicap sound efforts at reform, nor is it intended to have this effect." *Miranda* v. *Arizona, supra,* at 467.

V.

We come now to the question whether the denial of Wade's motion to strike the courtroom identification by the bank witnesses at trial because of the absence of his counsel at the lineup required, as the Court of Appeals held, the grant of a new trial at which such evidence is

[30] Thirty years ago Wigmore suggested a "scientific method" of pretrial identification "to reduce the risk of error hitherto inherent in such proceedings." Wigmore, The Science of Judicial Proof 541 (3d ed. 1937). Under this approach, at least 100 talking films would be prepared of men from various occupations, races, etc. Each would be photographed in a number of stock movements, with and without hat and coat, and would read aloud a standard passage. The suspect would be filmed in the same manner. Some 25 of the films would be shown in succession in a special projection room in which each witness would be provided an electric button which would activate a board backstage when pressed to indicate that the witness had identified a given person. Provision would be made for the degree of hesitancy in the identification to be indicated by the number of presses. *Id.,* at 540–541. Of course, the more systematic and scientific a process or proceeding, including one for purposes of identification, the less the impediment to reconstruction of the conditions bearing upon the reliability of that process or proceeding at trial. See discussion of fingerprint and like tests, Part III, *supra,* and of handwriting exemplars in *Gilbert* v. *California, supra.*

to be excluded. We do not think this disposition can be justified without first giving the Government the opportunity to establish by clear and convincing evidence that the in-court identifications were based upon observations of the suspect other than the lineup identification. See *Murphy* v. *Waterfront Commission,* 378 U. S. 52, 79, n. 18.[31] Where, as here, the admissibility of evidence of the lineup identification itself is not involved, a *per se* rule of exclusion of courtroom identification would be unjustified.[32] See *Nardone* v. *United States,* 308 U. S. 338, 341. A rule limited solely to the exclusion of testimony concerning identification at the lineup itself, without regard to admissibility of the courtroom identification, would render the right to counsel an empty one. The lineup is most often used, as in the present case, to crystallize the witnesses' identification of the defendant for future reference. We have already noted that the lineup identification will have that effect. The State may then rest upon the witnesses' unequivocal courtroom identification, and not mention the pretrial identification as part of the State's case at trial. Counsel is then in the predicament in which Wade's counsel found himself—realizing that possible unfairness at the lineup may be the sole means of attack upon the unequivocal courtroom identification, and having to probe in the dark

---

[31] See *Goldstein* v. *United States,* 316 U. S. 114, 124, n. 1 (Murphy, J., dissenting). "[A]fter an accused sustains the initial burden, imposed by *Nardone* v. *United States,* 308 U. S. 338, of proving to the satisfaction of the trial judge in the preliminary hearing that wire-tapping was unlawfully employed, as petitioners did here, it is only fair that the burden should then shift to the Government to convince the trial judge that its proof had an independent origin."

[32] We reach a contrary conclusion in *Gilbert* v. *California, supra,* as to the admissibility of the witness' testimony that he also identified the accused at the lineup.

in an attempt to discover and reveal unfairness, while bolstering the government witness' courtroom identification by bringing out and dwelling upon his prior identification. Since counsel's presence at the lineup would equip him to attack not only the lineup identification but the courtroom identification as well, limiting the impact of violation of the right to counsel to exclusion of evidence only of identification at the lineup itself disregards a critical element of that right.

We think it follows that the proper test to be applied in these situations is that quoted in *Wong Sun* v. *United States,* 371 U. S. 471, 488, " '[W]hether, granting establishment of the primary illegality, the evidence to which instant objection is made has been come at by exploitation of that illegality or instead by means sufficiently distinguishable to be purged of the primary taint.' Maguire, Evidence of Guilt 221 (1959)." See also *Hoffa* v. *United States,* 385 U. S. 293, 309. Application of this test in the present context requires consideration of various factors; for example, the prior opportunity to observe the alleged criminal act, the existence of any discrepancy between any pre-lineup description and the defendant's actual description, any identification prior to lineup of another person, the identification by picture of the defendant prior to the lineup, failure to identify the defendant on a prior occasion, and the lapse of time between the alleged act and the lineup identification. It is also relevant to consider those facts which, despite the absence of counsel, are disclosed concerning the conduct of the lineup.[33]

---

[33] Thus it is not the case that "[i]t matters not how well the witness knows the suspect, whether the witness is the suspect's mother, brother, or long-time associate, and no matter how long or well the witness observed the perpetrator at the scene of the crime." Such factors will have an important bearing upon the true basis of

We doubt that the Court of Appeals applied the proper test for exclusion of the in-court identification of the two witnesses. The court stated that "it cannot be said with any certainty that they would have recognized appellant at the time of trial if this intervening lineup had not occurred," and that the testimony of the two witnesses "may well have been colored by the illegal procedure [and] was prejudicial." 358 F. 2d, at 560. Moreover, the court was persuaded, in part, by the "compulsory verbal responses made by Wade at the instance of the Special Agent." *Ibid.* This implies the erroneous holding that Wade's privilege against self-incrimination was violated so that the denial of counsel required exclusion.

On the record now before us we cannot make the determination whether the in-court identifications had an independent origin. This was not an issue. at trial, although there is some evidence relevant to a determination. That inquiry is most properly made in the District Court. We therefore think the appropriate procedure to be followed is to vacate the conviction pending a hearing to determine whether the in-court identifications had an independent source, or whether, in any event, the introduction of the evidence was harmless error, *Chapman* v. *California,* 386 U. S. 18, and for the District Court to reinstate the conviction or order a new trial, as may be proper. See *United States* v. *Shotwell Mfg. Co.,* 355 U. S. 233, 245–246.

the witness' in-court identification. Moreover, the State's inability to bolster the witness' courtroom identification by introduction of the lineup identification .itself, see *Gilbert* v. *California, supra,* will become less significant the more the evidence of other opportunities of the witness to observe the defendant. · Thus where the witness is a "kidnap victim who has lived for days with his abductor" the value to the State of admission of the lineup identification is indeed marginal, and such identification would be a mere formality.

The judgment of the Court of Appeals is vacated and the case is remanded to that court with direction to enter a new judgment vacating the conviction and remanding the case to the District Court for further proceedings consistent with this opinion.

It is so ordered.

THE CHIEF JUSTICE joins the opinion of the Court except for Part I, from which he dissents for the reasons expressed in the opinion of MR. JUSTICE FORTAS.

MR. JUSTICE DOUGLAS joins the opinion of the Court except for Part I. On that phase of the case he adheres to the dissenting views in *Schmerber* v. *California,* 384 U. S. 757, 772–779, that compulsory lineup violates the privilege against self-incrimination contained in the Fifth Amendment.

MR. JUSTICE CLARK, concurring.

With reference to the lineup point involved in this case I cannot, for the life of me, see why a lineup is not a critical stage of the prosecution. Identification of the suspect—a prerequisite to establishment of guilt—occurs at this stage, and with *Miranda* v. *Arizona,* 384 U. S. 436 (1966), on the books, the requirement of the presence of counsel arises, unless waived by the suspect. I dissented in *Miranda* but I am bound by it now, as we all are. *Schmerber* v. *California,* 384 U. S. 757 (1966), precludes petitioner's claim of self-incrimination. I therefore join the opinion of the Court.

MR. JUSTICE BLACK, dissenting in part and concurring in part.

On March 23, 1965, respondent Wade was indicted for robbing a bank; on April 2, he was arrested; and on April 26, the court appointed a lawyer to represent him.

Fifteen days later, while Wade was still in custody, an FBI agent took him and several other prisoners into a room at the courthouse, directed each to participate in a lineup wearing strips of tape on his face and to speak the words used by the robber at the bank. This was all done in order to let the bank employee witnesses look at Wade for identification purposes. Wade's lawyer was not notified of nor present at the lineup to protect his client's interests. At Wade's trial, two bank employees identified him in the courtroom. Wade objected to this testimony, when, on cross-examination, his counsel elicited from these witnesses the fact that they had seen Wade in the lineup. He contended that by forcing him to participate in the lineup, wear strips of tape on his face, and repeat the words used by the robber, all without counsel, the Government had (1) compelled him to be a witness against himself in violation of the Fifth Amendment, and (2) deprived him of the assistance of counsel for his defense in violation of the Sixth Amendment.

The Court in Part I of its opinion rejects Wade's Fifth Amendment contention. From that I dissent. In Parts II–IV of its opinion, the Court sustains Wade's claim of denial of right to counsel in the out-of-court lineup, and in that I concur. In Part V, the Court remands the case to the District Court to consider whether the courtroom identification of Wade was the fruit of the illegal lineup, and if it was, to grant him a new trial unless the court concludes that the courtroom identification was harmless error. I would reverse the Court of Appeals' reversal of Wade's conviction, but I would not remand for further proceedings. Since the prosecution did not use the out-of-court lineup identification against Wade at his trial, I believe the conviction should be affirmed.

I.

In rejecting Wade's claim that his privilege against self-incrimination was violated by compelling him to appear in the lineup wearing the tape and uttering the words given him by the police, the Court relies on the recent holding in *Schmerber* v. *California*, 384 U. S. 757. In that case the Court held that taking blood from a man's body against his will in order to convict him of a crime did not compel him to be a witness against himself. I dissented from that holding, 384 U. S., at 773, and still dissent. The Court's reason for its holding was that the sample of Schmerber's blood taken in order to convict him of crime was neither "testimonial" nor "communicative" evidence. I think it was both. It seems quite plain to me that the Fifth Amendment's Self-incrimination Clause was designed to bar the Government from forcing any person to supply proof of his own crime, precisely what Schmerber was forced to do when he was forced to supply his blood. The Government simply took his blood against his will and over his counsel's protest for the purpose of convicting him of crime. So here, having Wade in its custody awaiting trial to see if he could or would be convicted of crime, the Government forced him to stand in a lineup, wear strips on his face, and speak certain words, in order to make it possible for government witnesses to identify him as a criminal. Had Wade been compelled to utter these or any other words in open court, it is plain that he would have been entitled to a new trial because of having been compelled to be a witness against himself. Being forced by the Government to help convict himself and to supply evidence against himself by talking outside the courtroom is equally violative of his constitutional right not to be compelled to be a witness against himself. Consequently, because of this violation of the Fifth Amendment, and not because of my own personal view that the Government's conduct was "unfair," "prejudicial," or "improper," I would prohibit the prosecution's use of lineup identification at trial.

II.

I agree with the Court, in large part because of the reasons it gives, that failure to notify Wade's counsel that Wade was to be put in a lineup by government officers and to be forced to talk and wear tape on his face denied Wade the right to counsel in violation of the Sixth Amendment. Once again, my reason for this conclusion is solely the Sixth Amendment's guarantee that "the accused shall enjoy the right . . . to have the Assistance of Counsel for his defence." As this Court's opinion points out, "[t]he plain wording of this guarantee thus encompasses counsel's assistance whenever necessary to assure a meaningful 'defence.'" And I agree with the Court that a lineup is a "critical stage" of the criminal proceedings against an accused, because it is a stage at which the Government makes use of his custody to obtain crucial evidence against him. Besides counsel's presence at the lineup being necessary to protect the defendant's specific constitutional rights to confrontation and the assistance of counsel at the trial itself, the assistance of counsel at the lineup is also necessary to protect the defendant's in-custody assertion of his privilege against self-incrimination, *Miranda* v. *Arizona*, 384 U. S. 436, for, contrary to the Court, I believe that counsel may advise the defendant not to participate in the lineup or to participate only under certain conditions.

I agree with the Court that counsel's presence at the lineup is necessary to protect the accused's right to a "fair trial," only if by "fair trial" the Court means a trial in accordance with the "Law of the Land" as specifically set out in the Constitution. But there are implications in the Court's opinion that by a "fair trial" the Court means a trial which a majority of this Court deems to be "fair" and that a lineup is a "critical stage" only because the Court, now assessing the "innumerable dangers" which inhere in it, thinks it is such. That these implications are justified is evidenced by the Court's suggestion that "[l]egislative or other regulations . . . which eliminate the risks of abuse . . . at lineup proceedings . . . may also remove the basis for regarding the stage as 'critical.'" And it is clear from the Court's opinion in *Gilbert* v. *California, post,* p. 263, that it is willing to make the Sixth Amendment's guarantee of right to counsel dependent on the Court's own view of whether a particular stage of the proceedings—though "critical" in the sense of the prosecution's gathering of evidence—is "critical" to the Court's own view of a "fair trial." I am wholly unwilling to make the specific constitutional right of counsel dependent on judges' vague and transitory notions of fairness and their equally transitory, though thought to be empirical, assessment of the "risk that . . . counsel's absence . . . might derogate from . . . [a defendant's] right to a fair trial." *Ante,* at 228. See *Pointer* v. *Texas,* 380 U. S. 400, 412 (concurring opinion of Goldberg, J.).

III.

I would reverse Wade's conviction without further ado had the prosecution at trial made use of his lineup identification either in place of courtroom identification or to bolster in a harmful manner crucial courtroom identification. But the prosecution here did neither of these things. After prosecution witnesses under oath identified Wade in the courtroom, it was the defense, and not the prosecution, which brought out the prior lineup identification. While stating that "a *per se* rule of exclusion of courtroom identification would be unjustified," the Court, nevertheless, remands this case for "a hearing to determine whether the in-court identifications had an independent source," or were the tainted fruits of the invalidly conducted lineup. From this holding I dissent.

In the first place, even if this Court has power to establish such a rule of evidence, I think the rule fashioned by the Court is unsound. The "tainted fruit" determination required by the Court involves more than considerable difficulty. I think it is practically impossible. How is a witness capable of probing the recesses of his mind to draw a sharp line between a courtroom identification due exclusively to an earlier lineup and a courtroom identification due to memory not based on the lineup? What kind of "clear and convincing evidence" can the prosecution offer to prove upon what particular events memories resulting in an in-court identification rest? How long will trials be delayed while judges turn psychologists to probe the subconscious minds of witnesses? All these questions are posed but not answered by the Court's opinion. In my view, the Fifth and Sixth Amendments are satisfied if the prosecution is precluded from using lineup identification as either an alternative to or corroboration of courtroom identification. If the prosecution does neither and its witnesses under oath identify the defendant in the courtroom, then I can find no justification for stopping the trial in midstream to hold a lengthy "tainted fruit" hearing. The fact of and circumstances surrounding a prior lineup identification might be used by the defense to impeach the credibility of the in-court identifications, but not to exclude them completely.

But more important, there is no constitutional provision upon which I can rely that directly or by implication gives this Court power to establish what amounts to a constitutional rule of evidence to govern, not only the Federal Government, but the States in their trial of state crimes under state laws in state courts. See *Gilbert* v. *California, supra.* The Constitution deliberately reposed in States very broad power to create and to try crimes according to their own rules and policies. *Spencer* v. *Texas,* 385 U. S. 554. Before being deprived of this power, the least that they can ask is that we should be able to point to a federal constitutional provision that either by express language or by necessary implication grants us the power to fashion this novel rule of evidence to govern their criminal trials. Cf. *Berger* v. *New York, ante,* p. 70 (BLACK, J., dissenting). Neither *Nardone* v. *United States,* 308 U. S. 338, nor *Wong Sun* v. *United States,* 371 U. S. 471, both federal cases and both decided "in other contexts," supports what the Court demands of the States today.

Perhaps the Court presumes to write this constitutional rule of evidence on the basis of the Fourteenth Amendment's Due Process Clause. This is not the time or place to consider that claim. Suffice it for me to say briefly that I find no such authority in the Due Process Clause. It undoubtedly provides that a person must be tried in accordance with the "Law of the Land." Consequently, it violates due process to try a person in a way prohibited by the Fourth, Fifth, or Sixth Amendments of our written Constitution. But I have never been able to subscribe to the dogma that the Due Process Clause empowers this Court to declare any law, including a rule of evidence, unconstitutional which it believes is contrary to tradition, decency, fundamental justice, or any of the other wide-meaning words used by judges to claim power under the Due Process Clause. See, *e. g., Rochin* v. *California,* 342 U. S. 165. I have an abiding idea that if the Framers had wanted to let judges write the Constitution on any such day-to-day beliefs of theirs, they would have said so instead of so carefully defining their grants and prohibitions in a written constitution.

With no more authority than the Due Process Clause
I am wholly unwilling to tell the state or federal courts
that the United States Constitution forbids them to allow
courtroom identification without the prosecution's first
proving that the identification does not rest in whole or
in part on an illegal lineup. Should I do so, I would feel
that we are deciding what the Constitution is, not from
what it says, but from what we think it would have been
wise for the Framers to put in it. That to me would
be "judicial activism" at its worst. I would leave the
States and Federal Government free to decide their own
rules of evidence. That, I believe, is their constitutional
prerogative.

I would affirm Wade's conviction.

MR. JUSTICE WHITE, whom MR. JUSTICE HARLAN and
MR. JUSTICE STEWART join, dissenting in part and concurring in part.

The Court has again propounded a broad constitutional
rule barring use of a wide spectrum of relevant and probative evidence, solely because a step in its ascertainment
or discovery occurs outside the presence of defense counsel. This was the approach of the Court in *Miranda* v.
Arizona, 384 U. S. 436. I objected then to what I thought
was an uncritical and doctrinaire approach without satisfactory factual foundation. I have much the same view
of the present ruling and therefore dissent from the judgment and from Parts II, IV, and V of the Court's opinion.

The Court's opinion is far-reaching. It proceeds first
by creating a new *per se* rule of constitutional law: a
criminal suspect cannot be subjected to a pretrial identification process in the absence of his counsel without
violating the Sixth Amendment. If he is, the State
may not buttress a later courtroom identification of the
witness by any reference to the previous identification.
Furthermore, the courtroom identification is not admis-

sible at all unless the State can establish by clear and
convincing proof that the testimony is not the fruit of
the earlier identification made in the absence of defendant's counsel—admittedly a heavy burden for the State
and probably an impossible one. To all intents and
purposes, courtroom identifications are barred if pretrial identifications have occurred without counsel being
present.

The rule applies to any lineup, to any other techniques
employed to produce an identification and *a fortiori* to
a face-to-face encounter between the witness and the
suspect alone, regardless of when the identification occurs,
in time or place, and whether before or after indictment
or information. It matters not how well the witness
knows the suspect, whether the witness is the suspect's
mother, brother, or long-time associate, and no matter
how long or well the witness observed the perpetrator
at the scene of the crime. The kidnap victim who has
lived for days with his abductor is in the same category
as the witness who has had only a fleeting glimpse of the
criminal. Neither may identify the suspect without
defendant's counsel being present. The same strictures
apply regardless of the number of other witnesses who
positively identify the defendant and regardless of the
corroborative evidence showing that it was the defendant
who had committed the crime.

The premise for the Court's rule is not the general
unreliability of eyewitness identifications nor the difficulties inherent in observation, recall, and recognition.
The Court assumes a narrower evil as the basis for its
rule—improper police suggestion which contributes to
erroneous identifications. The Court apparently believes
that improper police procedures are so widespread that
a broad prophylactic rule must be laid down, requiring
the presence of counsel at all pretrial identifications, in

order to detect recurring instances of police misconduct.[1]
I do not share this pervasive distrust of all official investigations. None of the materials the Court relies upon
supports it.[2] Certainly, I would bow to solid fact, but
the Court quite obviously does not have before it any
reliable, comprehensive survey of current police practices
on which to base its new rule. Until it does, the Court
should avoid excluding relevant evidence from state
criminal trials. Cf. *Washington* v. *Texas, ante,* p. 14.

The Court goes beyond assuming that a great majority
of the country's police departments are following improper practices at pretrial identifications. To find the
lineup a "critical" stage of the proceeding and to exclude
identifications made in the absence of counsel, the Court
must also assume that police "suggestion," if it occurs
at all, leads to erroneous rather than accurate identifications and that reprehensible police conduct will have
an unavoidable and largely undiscoverable impact on the
trial. This in turn assumes that there is now no adequate
source from which defense counsel can learn about the
circumstances of the pretrial identification in order to
place before the jury all of the considerations which
should enter into an appraisal of courtroom identification

---

[1] Yet in *Stovall* v. *Denno, post,* p. 293, the Court recognizes that
improper police conduct in the identification process has not been
so widespread as to justify full retroactivity for its new rule.

[2] In *Miranda* v. *Arizona,* 384 U. S. 436, 449, the Court noted that
O'Hara, Fundamentals of Criminal Investigation (1956) is a text
that has enjoyed extensive use among law enforcement agencies and
among students of police science. The quality of the work was said
to rest on the author's long service as observer, lecturer in police
science, and work as a federal crime investigator. O'Hara does not
suggest that the police should or do use identification machinery
improperly; instead he argues for techniques that would increase
the reliability of eyewitness identifications, and there is no reason
to suggest that O'Hara's views are not shared and practiced by the
majority of police departments throughout the land.

evidence. But these are treacherous and unsupported assumptions,[3] resting as they do on the notion that the defendant will not be aware, that the police and the witnesses will forget or prevaricate, that defense counsel will be unable to bring out the truth and that neither jury, judge, nor appellate court is a sufficient safeguard against unacceptable police conduct occurring at a pretrial identification procedure. I am unable to share the Court's view of the willingness of the police and the ordinary citizen-witness to dissemble, either with respect to the identification of the defendant or with respect to the circumstances surrounding a pretrial identification.

There are several striking aspects to the Court's holding. First, the rule does not bar courtroom identifications where there have been no previous identifications in the presence of the police, although when identified in the courtroom, the defendant is known to be in custody and charged with the commission of a crime. Second, the Court seems to say that if suitable legislative standards were adopted for the conduct of pretrial identifications, thereby lessening the hazards in such con-

---

[3] The instant case and its companions, *Gilbert* v. *California, post,* p. 263, and *Stovall* v. *Denno, post,* p. 293, certainly lend no support to the Court's assumptions. The police conduct deemed improper by the Court in the three cases seems to have come to light at trial in the ordinary course of events. One can ask what more counsel would have learned at the pretrial identifications that would have been relevant for truth determination at trial. When the Court premises its constitutional rule on police conduct so subtle as to defy description and subsequent disclosure it deals in pure speculation. If police conduct is intentionally veiled, the police will know about it, and I am unwilling to speculate that defense counsel at trial will be unable to reconstruct the known circumstances of the pretrial identification. And if the "unknown" influence on identifications is "innocent," the Court's general premise evaporates and the problem is simply that of the inherent shortcomings of eye-witness testimony.

frontations, it would not insist on the presence of counsel.
But if this is true, why does not the Court simply fashion
what it deems to be constitutionally acceptable procedures for the authorities to follow? Certainly the
Court is correct in suggesting that the new rule will be
wholly inapplicable where police departments themselves
have established suitable safeguards.

Third, courtroom identification may be barred, absent
counsel at a prior identification, regardless of the extent
of counsel's information concerning the circumstances of
the previous confrontation between witness and defendant—apparently even if there were recordings or sound-
movies of the events as they occurred. But if the rule
is premised on the defendant's right to have his counsel
know, there seems little basis for not accepting other
means to inform. A disinterested observer, recordings,
photographs—any one of them would seem adequate to
furnish the basis for a meaningful cross-examination
of the eyewitness who identifies the defendant in the
courtroom.

I share the Court's view that the criminal trial, at the
very least, should aim at truthful factfinding, including
accurate eyewitness identifications. I doubt, however,
on the basis of our present information, that the tragic
mistakes which have occurred in criminal trials are as
much the product of improper police conduct as they are
the consequence of the difficulties inherent in eyewitness
testimony and in resolving evidentiary conflicts by court
or jury. I doubt that the Court's new rule will obviate
these difficulties, or that the situation will be measurably
improved by inserting defense counsel into the investigative processes of police departments everywhere.

But, it may be asked, what possible state interest
militates against requiring the presence of defense counsel at lineups? After all, the argument goes, he *may*
do some good, he *may* upgrade the quality of identification evidence in state courts and he can scarcely do any

harm. Even if true, this is a feeble foundation for fastening an ironclad constitutional rule upon state criminal procedures. Absent some reliably established constitutional violation, the processes by which the States enforce their criminal laws are their own prerogative. The States *do* have an interest in conducting their own affairs, an interest which cannot be displaced simply by saying that there are no valid arguments with respect to the merits of a federal rule emanating from this Court.

Beyond this, however, requiring counsel at pretrial identifications as an invariable rule trenches on other valid state interests. One of them is its concern with the prompt and efficient enforcement of its criminal laws. Identifications frequently take place after arrest but before indictment or information is filed. The police may have arrested a suspect on probable cause but may still have the wrong man. Both the suspect and the State have every interest in a prompt identification at that stage, the suspect in order to secure his immediate release and the State because prompt and early identification enhances *accurate* identification and because it must know whether it is on the right investigative track. Unavoidably, however, the absolute rule requiring the presence of counsel will cause significant delay and it may very well result in no pretrial identification at all. Counsel must be appointed and a time arranged convenient for him and the witnesses. Meanwhile, it may be necessary to file charges against the suspect who may then be released on bail, in the federal system very often on his own recognizance, with neither the State nor the defendant having the benefit of a properly conducted identification procedure.

Nor do I think the witnesses themselves can be ignored. They will now be required to be present at the convenience of counsel rather than their own. Many may be much less willing to participate if the identification stage is transformed into an adversary proceeding not under the control of a judge. Others may fear for their own safety if their identity is known at an early date, especially when there is no way of knowing until the lineup occurs whether or not the police really have the right man.[4]

Finally, I think the Court's new rule is vulnerable in terms of its own unimpeachable purpose of increasing the reliability of identification testimony.

Law enforcement officers have the obligation to convict the guilty and to make sure they do not convict the innocent. They must be dedicated to making the criminal trial a procedure for the ascertainment of the true facts surrounding the commission of the crime.[5] To this extent, our so-called adversary system is not adversary at all; nor should it be. But defense counsel has no comparable obligation to ascertain or present the truth. Our system assigns him a different mission. He must

---

[4] I would not have thought that the State's interest regarding its sources of identification is any less than its interest in protecting informants, especially those who may aid in identification but who will not be used as witnesses. See *McCray* v. *Illinois,* 386 U. S. 300.

[5] "The United States Attorney is the representative not of an ordinary party to a controversy, but of a sovereignty whose obligation to govern impartially is as compelling as its obligation to govern at all; and whose interest, therefore, in a criminal prosecution is not that it shall win a case, but that justice shall be done. As such, he is in a peculiar and very definite sense the servant of the law, the twofold aim of which is that guilt shall not escape or innocence suffer. He may prosecute with earnestness and vigor— indeed, he should do so. But, while he may strike hard blows, he is not at liberty to strike foul ones. It is as much his duty to refrain from improper methods calculated to produce a wrongful conviction as it is to use every legitimate means to bring about a just one." *Berger* v. *United States,* 295 U. S. 78, 88. See also *Mooney* v. *Holohan,* 294 U. S. 103; *Pyle* v. *Kansas,* 317 U. S. 213; *Alcorta* v. *Texas,* 355 U. S. 28; *Napue* v. *Illinois,* 360 U. S. 264; *Brady* v. *Maryland,* 373 U. S. 83; *Giles* v. *Maryland,* 386 U. S. 66; *Miller* v. *Pate,* 386 U. S. 1.

UNITED STATES *v.* WADE.

be and is interested in not convicting the innocent, but, absent a voluntary plea of guilty, we also insist that he defend his client whether he is innocent or guilty. The State has the obligation to present the evidence. Defense counsel need present nothing, even if he knows what the truth is. He need furnish no witnesses to the police, reveal any confidences of his client, nor furnish any other information to help the prosecution's case. If he can confuse a witness, even a truthful one, or make him appear at a disadvantage, unsure or indecisive, that will be his normal course.[6] Our interest in not con-

---

[6] One point of view about the role of the courtroom lawyer appears in Frank, Courts on Trial 82–83. "What is the role of the lawyers in bringing the evidence before the trial court? As you may learn by reading any one of a dozen or more handbooks on how to try a law-suit, an experienced lawyer uses all sorts of stratagems to minimize the effect on the judge or jury of testimony disadvantageous to his client, even when the lawyer has no doubt of the accuracy and honesty of that testimony. . . . If such a witness happens to be timid, frightened by the unfamiliarity of court-room ways, the lawyer, in his cross-examination, plays on that weakness, in order to confuse the witness and make it appear that he is concealing significant facts. Longenecker, in his book *Hints On The Trial of a Law Suit* (a book endorsed by the great Wigmore), in writing of the 'truthful, honest, over-cautious' witness, tells how 'a skilful advocate by a rapid cross-examination may ruin the testimony of such a witness.' The author does not even hint any disapproval of that accomplishment. Longenecker's and other similar books recommend that a lawyer try to prod an irritable but honest 'adverse' witness into displaying his undesirable characteristics in their most unpleasant form, in order to discredit him with the judge or jury. 'You may,' writes Harris, 'sometimes destroy the effect of an adverse witness by making him appear more hostile than he really is. You may make him exaggerate or unsay something and say it again.' Taft says that a clever cross-examiner, dealing with an honest but egotistic witness, will 'deftly tempt the witness to indulge in his propensity for exaggeration, so as to make him "hang himself." 'And thus,' adds Taft, 'it may happen that not only is the value of his testimony lost, but the side which produces him

victing the innocent permits counsel to put the State
to its proof, to put the State's case in the worst possible
light, regardless of what he thinks or knows to be the
truth. Undoubtedly there are some limits which defense counsel must observe [7] but more often than not,
defense counsel will cross-examine a prosecution witness,
and impeach him if he can, even if he thinks the witness is telling the truth, just as he will attempt to destroy a witness who he thinks is lying. In this respect,
as part of our modified adversary system and as part of
the duty imposed on the most honorable defense counsel, we countenance or require conduct which in many
instances has little, if any, relation to the search for
truth.

I would not extend this system, at least as it presently
operates, to police investigations and would not require
counsel's presence at pretrial identification procedures.
Counsel's interest is in not having his client placed at the
scene of the crime, regardless of his whereabouts. Some
counsel may advise their clients to refuse to make any

suffers for seeking aid from such a source'—although, I would add,
that may be the only source of evidence of a fact on which the
decision will turn.

" 'An intimidating manner in putting questions,' writes Wigmore,
'may so coerce or disconcert the witness that his answers do not
represent his actual knowledge on the subject. So also, questions
which in form or subject cause embarrassment, shame or anger in
the witness may unfairly lead him to such demeanor or utterances
that the impression produced by his statements does not do justice
to its real testimonial value.' "

[7] See the materials collected in c. 3 of Countryman & Finman,
The Lawyer in Modern Society; Joint Committee on Continuing
Legal Education of American Law Institute and the American Bar
Association, The Problem of a Criminal Defense 1–46 (1961);
Stovall, Aspects of the Advocate's Dual Responsibility, 22 The
Alabama Lawyer 66; Gold, Split Loyalty: An Ethical Problem for
the Criminal Defense Lawyer, 14 Clev.-Mar. L. Rev. 65; Symposium
on Professional Ethics, 64 Mich. L. Rev. 1469–1498.

movements or to speak any words in a lineup or even
to appear in one. To that extent the impact on truthful factfinding is quite obvious. Others will not only
observe what occurs and develop possibilities for later
cross-examination but will hover over witnesses and begin their cross-examination then, menacing truthful fact-
finding as thoroughly as the Court fears the police now
do. Certainly there is an implicit invitation to counsel
to suggest rules for the lineup and to manage and produce it as best he can. I therefore doubt that the Court's
new rule, at least absent some clearly defined limits on
counsel's role, will measurably contribute to more reliable
pretrial identifications. My fears are that it will have
precisely the opposite result. It may well produce fewer
convictions, but that is hardly a proper measure of its
long-run acceptability. In my view, the State is entitled
to investigate and develop its case outside the presence
of defense counsel. This includes the right to have
private conversations with identification witnesses, just
as defense counsel may have his own consultations with
these and other witnesses without having the prosecutor
present.

Whether today's judgment would be an acceptable exercise of supervisory power over federal courts is another question. But as a constitutional matter, the
judgment in this case is erroneous and although I concur
in Parts I and III of the Court's opinion I respectfully
register this dissent.

MR. JUSTICE FORTAS, with whom THE CHIEF JUSTICE
and MR. JUSTICE DOUGLAS join, concurring in part and
dissenting in part.

1. I agree with the Court that the exhibition of the
person of the accused at a lineup is not itself a violation of the privilege against self-incrimination. In
itself, it is no more subject to constitutional objection

than the exhibition of the person of the accused in the courtroom for identification purposes. It is an incident of the State's power to arrest, and a reasonable and justifiable aspect of the State's custody resulting from arrest. It does not require that the accused take affirmative, volitional action, but only that, having been duly arrested he may be seen for identification purposes. It is, however, a "critical stage" in the prosecution, and I agree with the Court that the opportunity to have counsel present must be made available.

2. In my view, however, the accused may not be compelled in a lineup to speak the words uttered by the person who committed the crime. I am confident that it could not be compelled in court. It cannot be compelled in a lineup. It is more than passive, mute assistance to the eyes of the victim or of witnesses. It is the kind of volitional act—the kind of forced cooperation by the accused—which is within the historical perimeter of the privilege against compelled self-incrimination.

Our history and tradition teach and command that an accused may stand mute. The privilege means just that; not less than that. According to the Court, an accused may be jailed—indefinitely—until he is willing to say, for an identifying audience, whatever was said in the course of the commission of the crime. Presumably this would include, "Your money or your life"—or perhaps, words of assault in a rape case. This is intolerable under our constitutional system.

I completely agree that the accused must be advised of and given the right to counsel before a lineup—and I join in that part of the Court's opinion; but this is an empty right unless we mean to insist upon the accused's fundamental constitutional immunities. One of these is that the accused may not be compelled to speak. To compel him to speak would violate the privilege against self-incrimination, which is incorporated in the Fifth Amendment.

This great privilege is not merely a shield for the accused. It is also a prescription of technique designed to guide the State's investigation. History teaches us that self-accusation is an unreliable instrument of detection, apt to inculpate the innocent-but-weak and to enable the guilty to escape. But this is not the end of the story. The privilege historically goes to the roots of democratic and religious principle. It prevents the debasement of the citizen which would result from compelling him to "accuse" himself before the power of the state. The roots of the privilege are deeper than the rack and the screw used to extort confessions. They go to the nature of a free man and to his relationship to the state.

An accused cannot be compelled to utter the words spoken by the criminal in the course of the crime. I thoroughly disagree with the Court's statement that such compulsion does not violate the Fifth Amendment. The Court relies upon *Schmerber* v. *California,* 384 U. S. 757 (1966), to support this. I dissented in *Schmerber,* but if it were controlling here, I should, of course, acknowledge its binding effect unless we were prepared to overrule it. But *Schmerber* which authorized the forced extraction of blood from the veins of an unwilling human being, did not compel the person actively to cooperate—to accuse himself by a volitional act which differs only in degree from compelling him to act out the crime, which, I assume, would be rebuffed by the Court. It is the latter feature which places the compelled utterance by the accused squarely within the history and noble purpose of the Fifth Amendment's commandment.

To permit *Schmerber* to apply in any respect beyond its holding is, in my opinion, indefensible. To permit its insidious doctrine to extend beyond the invasion of the body, which it permits, to compulsion of the will of a man, is to deny and defy a precious part of our historical faith and to discard one of the most profoundly cherished instruments by which we have established the freedom and dignity of the individual. We should not so alter the balance between the rights of the individual and of the state, achieved over centuries of conflict.

3. While the Court holds that the accused must be advised of and given the right to counsel at the lineup, it makes the privilege meaningless in this important respect. Unless counsel has been waived or, being present, has not objected to the accused's utterance of words used in the course of committing the crime, to compel such an utterance is constitutional error.*

Accordingly, while I join the Court in requiring vacating of the judgment below for a determination as to whether the identification of respondent was based upon factors independent of the lineup, I would do so not only because of the failure to offer counsel before the lineup but also because of the violation of respondent's Fifth Amendment rights.

---

*While it is conceivable that legislation might provide a meticulous lineup procedure which would *satisfy* constitutional requirements, I do not agree with the Court that this would "remove the basis for regarding the [lineup] stage as 'critical.'"

GILBERT v. CALIFORNIA.

GILBERT v. CALIFORNIA.

CERTIORARI TO THE SUPREME COURT OF CALIFORNIA.

No. 223.   Argued February 15–16, 1967.—Decided June 12, 1967.

Petitioner was convicted of armed robbery and the murder of a police officer. There were separate guilt and penalty stages of the trial before the same jury, which rendered a guilty verdict and imposed the death penalty. Petitioner alleges constitutional errors in the admission of testimony of some of the witnesses that they had also identified him at a lineup, which occurred 16 days after his indictment and after appointment of counsel, who was not notified, and in in-court identifications of other witnesses present at that lineup; in the admission of handwriting exemplars taken from him after arrest; and in the admission of a co-defendant's out-of-court statement mentioning petitioner's part in the crimes, which statement was held to have been improperly admitted against the co-defendant on the latter's appeal. Additionally, he alleges violation of his Fourth Amendment rights by police seizure of photographs of him from his locked apartment after a warrantless entry, and the admission of testimony identifying him from these photographs. *Held:*

1. The taking of handwriting exemplars did not violate petitioner's constitutional rights. Pp. 265–267.

   (a) The Fifth Amendment privilege against self-incrimination reaches compulsory communications, but a mere handwriting exemplar, in contrast with the content of what is written, is an identifying physical characteristic outside its protection. Pp. 266–267.

   (b) The taking of the exemplars was not a "critical" stage of the criminal proceedings entitling petitioner to the assistance of counsel; there is minimal risk that the absence of counsel might derogate from his right to a fair trial. P. 267.

2. Petitioner's request for reconsideration of *Delli Paoli* v. *United States*, 352 U. S. 232 (where the Court held that appropriate instructions to the jury would suffice to prevent prejudice to a defendant from references to him in a co-defendant's statement) in connection with his co-defendant's statement, need not be considered in view of the California Supreme Court's holding rejecting the *Delli Paoli* rationale but finding that any error to petitioner by the admission of the statement was harmless. Pp. 267–268.

3. A closer examination of the record than was possible when certiorari was granted reveals that the facts with respect to the search and seizure claim are not sufficiently clear to permit resolution of that question, and certiorari on this issue is vacated as improvidently granted. P. 269.

4. The admission of the in-court identifications of petitioner without first determining that they were not tainted by the illegal lineup procedure but were of independent origin was constitutional error. *United States* v. *Wade, ante,* p. 218. Pp. 269–274.

(a) Since the record does not permit an informed judgment whether the in-court identifications at the two stages of the trial had an independent source, petitioner is entitled only to a vacation of his conviction, pending proceedings in California courts allowing the State to establish that the in-court identifications had an independent source or that their introduction in evidence was harmless error. P. 272.

(b) With respect to testimony of witnesses that they identified petitioner at the lineup, which is a direct result of an illegal procedure, the State is not entitled to show that such testimony had an independent source but the California courts must, unless "able to declare a belief that it was harmless beyond a reasonable doubt," grant petitioner a new trial if such testimony was at the guilt stage, or grant appropriate relief if it was at the penalty stage. Pp. 272–274.

63 Cal. 2d 690, 408 P. 2d 365, vacated and remanded.

Luke McKissack argued the cause and filed briefs for petitioner.

Norman H. Sokolow, Deputy Attorney General of California, and *William E. James,* Assistant Attorney General, argued the cause for respondent. With them on the brief was *Thomas C. Lynch,* Attorney General.

Mr. Justice Brennan delivered the opinion of the Court.

This case was argued with *United States* v. *Wade, ante,* p. 218, and presents the same alleged constitutional error in the admission in evidence of in-court identifications there considered. In addition, petitioner alleges constitutional errors in the admission in evidence of testimony of some of the witnesses that they also identified him at the lineup, in the admission of handwriting exemplars taken from him after his arrest, and in the admission of a co-defendant's out-of-court statement mentioning petitioner's part in the crimes, which statement, on the co-defendant's appeal decided with petitioner's, was held to have been improperly admitted against the co-defendant. Finally, he alleges that his Fourth Amendment rights were violated by a police seizure of photographs of him from his locked apartment after entry without a search warrant, and the admission of testimony of witnesses that they identified him from those photographs within hours after the crime.

Petitioner was convicted in the Superior Court of California of the armed robbery of the Mutual Savings and Loan Association of Alhambra and the murder of a police officer who entered during the course of the robbery. There were separate guilt and penalty stages of the trial before the same jury, which rendered a guilty verdict and imposed the death penalty. The California Supreme Court affirmed, 63 Cal. 2d 690, 408 P. 2d 365. We granted certiorari, 384 U. S. 985, and set the case for argument with *Wade* and with *Stovall* v. *Denno, post,* p. 293. If our holding today in *Wade* is applied to this case, the issue whether admission of the in-court and lineup identifications is constitutional error which requires a new trial could be resolved on this record only after further proceedings in the California courts. We must therefore first determine whether petitioner's other contentions warrant any greater relief.

I.

THE HANDWRITING EXEMPLARS.

Petitioner was arrested in Philadelphia by an FBI agent and refused to answer questions about the Alhambra robbery without the advice of counsel. He later did answer questions of another agent about some Philadelphia robberies in which the robber used a handwritten note demanding that money be handed over to him, and during that interrogation gave the agent the handwriting exemplars. They were admitted in evidence at trial over objection that they were obtained in violation of petitioner's Fifth and Sixth Amendment rights. The California Supreme Court upheld admission of the exemplars on the sole ground that petitioner had waived any rights that he might have had not to furnish them. "[The agent] did not tell Gilbert that the exemplars would not be used in any other investigation. Thus, even if Gilbert believed that his exemplars would not be used in California, it does not appear that the authorities improperly induced such belief." 63 Cal. 2d, at 708, 408 P. 2d, at 376. The court did not, therefore, decide petitioner's constitutional claims.

We pass the question of waiver since we conclude that the taking of the exemplars violated none of petitioner's constitutional rights.

First. The taking of the exemplars did not violate petitioner's Fifth Amendment privilege against self-incrimination. The privilege reaches only compulsion of "an accused's communications, whatever form they might take, and the compulsion of responses which are also communications, for example, compliance with a subpoena to produce one's papers," and not "compulsion which makes a suspect or accused the source of 'real or physical evidence'. . . ." *Schmerber* v. *California,* 384 U. S. 757, 763-764. One's voice and handwriting are, of course, means of communication. It by no means follows, however, that every compulsion of an accused to use his voice or write compels a communication within the cover of the privilege. A mere handwriting exemplar, in contrast to the content of what is written, like the voice or body itself, is an identifying physical characteristic outside its protection. *United States* v. *Wade, supra,* at 222–223. No claim is made that the content of the exemplars was testimonial or communicative matter. Cf. *Boyd* v. *United States,* 116 U. S. 616.

Second. The taking of the exemplars was not a "critical" stage of the criminal proceedings entitling petitioner to the assistance of counsel. Putting aside the fact that the exemplars were taken before the indictment and appointment of counsel, there is minimal risk that the absence of counsel might derogate from his right to a fair trial. Cf. *United States* v. *Wade, supra.* If, for some reason, an unrepresentative exemplar is taken, this can be brought out and corrected through the adversary process at trial since the accused can make an unlimited number of additional exemplars for analysis and comparison by government and defense handwriting experts. Thus, "the accused has the opportunity for a meaningful confrontation of the [State's] case at trial through the ordinary processes of cross-examination of the [State's] expert [handwriting] witnesses and the presentation of the evidence of his own [handwriting] experts." *United States* v. *Wade, supra,* at 227–228.

II.

ADMISSION OF CO-DEFENDANT'S STATEMENT.

Petitioner contends that he was denied due process of law by the admission during the guilt stage of the trial of his accomplice's pretrial statement to the police which referred to petitioner 159 times in the course of reciting petitioner's role in the robbery and murder. The statement was inadmissible hearsay as to petitioner, and was held on King's aspect of this appeal to be improperly obtained from him and therefore to be inadmissible against him under California law. 63 Cal. 2d, at 699–701, 408 P. 2d, at 370–371.

Petitioner would have us reconsider *Delli Paoli* v. *United States*, 352 U. S. 232 (where the Court held that appropriate instructions to the jury would suffice to prevent prejudice to a defendant from the references to him in a co-defendant's statement), at least as applied to a case, as here, where the co-defendant gained a reversal because of the improper admission of the statement. We have no occasion to pass upon this contention. The California Supreme Court has rejected the *Delli Paoli* rationale, and relying at least in part on the reasoning of the *Delli Paoli* dissent, regards cautionary instructions as inadequate to cure prejudice. *People* v *Aranda*, 63 Cal. 2d 518, 407 P. 2d 265. The California court applied *Aranda* in this case but held that any error as to Gilbert in the admission of King's statement was harmless. The harmless error standard applied was that "there is no reasonable possibility that the error in admitting King's statements and testimony might have contributed to Gilbert's conviction," a standard derived by the court from our decision in *Fahy* v. *Connecticut*, 375 U. S. 85.[1] *Fahy* was the basis of our holding in *Chapman* v. *California*, 386 U. S. 18, and the standard applied by the California court satisfies the standard as defined in *Chapman*.

It may be that the California Supreme Court will review the application of its harmless error standard to King's statement if on the remand the State presses harmless error also in the introduction of the in-court and lineup identifications. However, this at best implies an ultimate application of *Aranda* and only confirms that petitioner's argument for reconsideration of *Delli Paoli* need not be considered at this time.

---

[1] The California Supreme Court also held that ". . . the erroneous admission of King's statements at the trial on the issue of guilt was not prejudicial on the question of Gilbert's penalty," again citing *Fahy*, 63 Cal. 2d, at 702, 408 P. 2d, at 372.

III.

The Search and Seizure Claim.

The California Supreme Court rejected Gilbert's challenge to the admission of certain photographs taken from his apartment pursuant to a warrantless search. The court justified the entry into the apartment under the circumstances on the basis of so-called "hot pursuit" and "exigent circumstances" exceptions to the warrant requirement. We granted certiorari to consider the important question of the extent to which such exceptions may permit warrantless searches without violation of the Fourth Amendment. A closer examination of the record than was possible when certiorari was granted reveals that the facts do not appear with sufficient clarity to enable us to decide that question. See Appendix to this opinion; compare *Warden* v. *Hayden,* 387 U. S. 294. We therefore vacate certiorari on this issue as improvidently granted. *The Monrosa* v. *Carbon Black Export, Inc.,* 359 U. S. 180, 184.

IV.

The In-court and Lineup Identifications.

Since none of the petitioner's other contentions warrants relief, the issue becomes what relief is required by application to this case of the principles today announced in *United States* v. *Wade, supra.*

Three eyewitnesses to the Alhambra crimes who identified Gilbert at the guilt stage of the trial had observed him at a lineup conducted without notice to his counsel in a Los Angeles auditorium 16 days after his indictment and after appointment of counsel. The manager of the apartment house in which incriminating evidence was found, and in which Gilbert allegedly resided, identified Gilbert in the courtroom and also testified, in substance, to her prior lineup identification on examination by the

State. Eight witnesses who identified him in the court-room at the penalty stage were not eyewitnesses to the Alhambra crimes but to other robberies allegedly committed by him. In addition to their in-court identifications, these witnesses also testified that they identified Gilbert at the same lineup.

The lineup was on a stage behind bright lights which prevented those in the line from seeing the audience. Upwards of 100 persons were in the audience, each an eyewitness to one of the several robberies charged to Gilbert. The record is otherwise virtually silent as to what occurred at the lineup.[2]

---

[2] The record in *Gilbert* v. *United States*, 366 F. 2d 923, involving the federal prosecutions of Gilbert, apparently contains many more details of what occurred at the lineup. The opinion of the Court of Appeals for the Ninth Circuit states, 366 F. 2d, at 935:

"The lineup occurred on March 26, 1964, after Gilbert had been indicted and had obtained counsel. It was held in an auditorium used for that purpose by the Los Angeles police. Some ten to thirteen prisoners were placed on a lighted stage. The witnesses were assembled in a darkened portion of the room, facing the stage and separated from it by a screen. They could see the prisoners but could not be seen by them. State and federal officers were also present and one of them acted as 'moderator' of the proceedings.

"Each man in the lineup was identified by number, but not by name. Each man was required to step forward into a marked circle, to turn, presenting both profiles as well as a face and back view, to walk, to put on or take off certain articles of clothing. When a man's number was called and he was directed to step into the circle, he was asked certain questions: where he was picked up, whether he owned a car, whether, when arrested, he was armed, where he lived. Each was also asked to repeat certain phrases, both in a loud and in a soft voice, phrases that witnesses to the crimes had heard the robbers use: 'Freeze, this is a stickup; this is a holdup; empty your cash drawer; this is a heist; don't anybody move.'

"Either while the men were on the stage, or after they were taken from it, it is not clear which, the assembled witnesses were asked if there were any that they would like to see again, and told that if they had doubts, now was the time to resolve them. Several

168

At the guilt stage, after the first witness, a cashier of the savings and loan association, identified Gilbert in the courtroom, defense counsel moved out of the presence of the jury to strike her testimony on the ground that she identified Gilbert at the pretrial lineup conducted in the absence of counsel in violation of the Sixth Amendment made applicable to the States by the Fourteenth Amendment. *Gideon* v. *Wainwright,* 372 U. S. 335. He requested a hearing outside the presence of the jury to present evidence supporting his claim that her in-court identification was, and others to be elicited by the State from other eyewitnesses would be, "predicated at least in large part upon their identification or purported identification of Mr. Gilbert at the showup . . . ." The trial judge denied the motion as premature. Defense counsel then elicited the fact of the cashier's lineup identification on cross-examination and again moved to strike her identification testimony. Without passing on the merits of the Sixth Amendment claim, the trial judge denied the motion on the ground that, assuming a violation, it would not in any event entitle Gilbert to suppression of the in-court identification. Defense counsel thereafter elicited the fact of lineup identifications from two other eyewitnesses who on direct examination identified Gilbert in the courtroom. Defense counsel unsuccessfully objected at the penalty stage, to the testimony of the eight witnesses to the other robberies that they identified Gilbert at the lineup.

gave the numbers of men they wanted to see, including Gilbert's. While the other prisoners were no longer present, Gilbert and 2 or 3 others were again put through a similar procedure. Some of the witnesses asked that a particular prisoner say a particular phrase, or walk a particular way. After the lineup, the witnesses talked to each other; it is not clear that they did so during the lineup. They did, however, in each other's presence, call out the numbers of men they could identify."

The admission of the in-court identifications without first determining that they were not tainted by the illegal lineup but were of independent origin was constitutional error. *United States* v. *Wade, supra.* We there held that a post-indictment pretrial lineup at which the accused is exhibited to identifying witnesses is a critical stage of the criminal prosecution; that police conduct of such a lineup without notice to and in the absence of his counsel denies the accused his Sixth Amendment right to counsel and calls in question the admissibility at trial of the in-court identifications of the accused by witnesses who attended the lineup. However, as in *Wade,* the record does not permit an informed judgment whether the in-court identifications at the two stages of the trial had an independent source. Gilbert is therefore entitled only to a vacation of his conviction pending the holding of such proceedings as the California Supreme Court may deem appropriate to afford the State the opportunity to establish that the in-court identifications had an independent source, or that their introduction in evidence was in any event harmless error.

Quite different considerations are involved as to the admission of the testimony of the manager of the apartment house at the guilt phase and of the eight witnesses at the penalty stage that they identified Gilbert at the lineup.[3] That testimony is the direct result of the illegal

---

[3] There is a split among the States concerning the admissibility of prior extrajudicial identifications, as independent evidence of identity, both by the witness and third parties present at the prior identification. See 71 ALR 2d 449. It has been held that the prior identification is hearsay, and, when admitted through the testimony of the identifier, is merely a prior consistent statement. The recent trend, however, is to admit the prior identification under the exception that admits as substantive evidence a prior communication by a witness who is available for cross-examination at trial. See 5 ALR 2d Later Case Service 1225–1228. That is the Cali-

lineup "come at by exploitation of [the primary] illegality." *Wong Sun* v. *United States,* 371 U. S. 471, 488. The State is therefore not entitled to an opportunity to show that that testimony had an independent source. Only a *per se* exclusionary rule as to such testimony can be an effective sanction to assure that law enforcement authorities will respect the accused's constitutional right to the presence of his counsel at the critical lineup. In the absence of legislative regulations adequate to avoid the hazards to a fair trial which inhere in lineups as presently conducted, the desirability of deterring the constitutionally objectionable practice must prevail over the undesirability of excluding relevant evidence. Cf. *Mapp* v. *Ohio,* 367 U. S. 643. That conclusion is buttressed by the consideration that the witness' testimony of his lineup identification will enhance the impact of his in-court identification on the jury and

fornia rule. In *People* v. *Gould,* 54 Cal. 2d 621, 626, 354 P. 2d 865, 867, the Court said:

"Evidence of an extrajudicial identification is admissible, not only to corroborate an identification made at the trial (*People* v. *Slobodion,* 31 Cal. 2d 555, 560 [191 P. 2d 1]), but as independent evidence of identity. Unlike other testimony that cannot be corroborated by proof of prior consistent statements unless it is first impeached . . . evidence of an extrajudicial identification is admitted regardless of whether the testimonial identification is impeached, because the earlier identification has greater probative value than an identification made in the courtroom after the suggestions of others and the circumstances of the trial may have intervened to create a fancied recognition in the witness' mind. . . . The failure of the witness to repeat the extrajudicial identification in court does not destroy its probative value, for such failure may be explained by loss of memory or other circumstances. The extrajudicial identification tends to connect the defendant with the crime, and the principal danger of admitting hearsay evidence is not present since the witness is available at the trial for cross-examination." New York deals with the subject in a statute. See N. Y. Code Crim. Proc. § 393–b.

seriously aggravate whatever derogation exists of the accused's right to a fair trial. Therefore, unless the California Supreme Court is "able to declare a belief that it was harmless beyond a reasonable doubt," *Chapman* v. *California,* 386 U. S. 18, 24, Gilbert will be entitled on remand to a new trial or, if no prejudicial error is found on the guilt stage but only in the penalty stage, to whatever relief California law affords where the penalty stage must be set aside.

The judgment of the California Supreme Court and the conviction are vacated, and the case is remanded to that court for further proceedings not inconsistent with this opinion.

It is so ordered.

THE CHIEF JUSTICE joins this opinion except for Part III, from which he dissents for the reasons expressed in the opinion of MR. JUSTICE DOUGLAS.

APPENDIX TO OPINION OF THE COURT.

Photographs of Gilbert introduced at the guilt stage of the trial had been viewed by eyewitnesses within hours after the robbery and murder. Officers had entered his apartment without a warrant and found them in an envelope on the top of a bedroom dresser. The envelope was of the kind customarily used in delivering developed prints, with the words "Marlboro Photo Studio" imprinted on it. The officers entered the apartment because of information given by an accomplice which led them to believe that one of the suspects might be inside the apartment. Assuming that the warrantless entry into the apartment was justified by the need immediately to search for the suspect, the issue remains whether the subsequent search was reasonably supported by those same exigent circumstances. If the envelope were come upon in the course of a search for the suspect, the answer might be different from that where it is come upon, even though in plain view, in the course of a general, indiscriminate search of closets, dressers, etc., after it is known that the occupant is absent. Still different considerations may be presented where officers, pursuing the suspect, find that he is absent from the apartment but conduct a limited search for suspicious objects in plain view which might aid in the pursuit. The problem with the record in the present case is that it could reasonably support any of these factual conclusions upon which our constitutional analysis should rest, and the trial court made no findings on the scope of search. The California Supreme Court, which had no more substantial basis upon which to resolve the conflict than this Court, stated that the photos were come upon "while the officers were looking through the apartment for their suspect . . . ." As will appear, a contrary conclusion is equally reasonable.

(1) Agent Schlatter testified that immediately upon entering the apartment which he put at "approximately 1:05," the officers made a quick search for the occupant, which took at most a minute, and that the continued presence of the officers became "a matter of a stake-out under the assumption that the person or persons involved would come back." He testified that the officer who found the photographs, Agent Crowley, had entered the apartment with him. Agent Schlatter's testimony might support the California Supreme Court's view of the scope of search; (2) Agent Crowley testified that he arrived within five minutes *after* Agent Schlatter, "around 1:30, give or take a few minutes either way," that the apartment had already been searched for the suspects, and that he was instructed "to look through the apartment for anything we could find that we could use to identify or continue the pursuit of this person

without conducting a detailed search." Crowley's further testimony was that the search, pursuant to which the photos were found, was limited in this manner, and that he merely inspected objects in plain sight which would aid in identification. He stated that a detailed search for guns and money was not conducted until after a warrant had issued over three hours later. (3) Agent Townsend said he arrived at the apartment "sometime between perhaps 1:30 and 2:00," and that "well within an hour" he, Agent Crowley, another agent and a local officer conducted a detailed search of the bedroom. He stated that they "looked through the bedroom closet and dresser and I think . . . the headstand." A substantial sum of money was found in the dresser. Townsend could not specifically say" whether Crowley was in the bedroom at the time the money was found. This testimony might support a finding that the officers were engaged in a general search of the bedroom at the time the photos were found.

The testimony of the agents concerning their time of arrival in the apartment is not inconsistent with any of the three possible conclusions as to the scope of search. Taking Townsend's testimony together with Crowley's, it can be concluded that the two arrived at about the same time. Agent Schlatter's testimony that Crowley arrived with him, at 1:05, however, supports a conclusion that Crowley had begun his activities before Townsend arrived. Then there is the testimony of Agent Kiel, who did not enter the apartment, that he obtained the photos while talking with the landlady "approximately 1:25 to 1:30," about the same time that both Crowley and Townsend testified they arrived. In sum, the testimony concerning the timing of the events surrounding the search is both approximate and itself contradictory.

GILBERT *v.* CALIFORNIA.

Mr. Justice Black, concurring in part and dissenting in part.

Petitioner was convicted of robbery and murder partially on the basis of handwriting samples he had given to the police while he was in custody without counsel and partially on evidence that he had been identified by eyewitnesses at a lineup identification ceremony held by California officers in a Los Angeles auditorium without notice to his counsel. The Court's opinion shows that the officers took Gilbert to the auditorium while he was a prisoner, formed a lineup of Gilbert and other persons, required each one to step forward, asked them certain questions, and required them to repeat certain phrases, while eyewitnesses to this and other crimes looked at them in efforts to identify them as the criminals. At his trial, Gilbert objected to the handwriting samples and to the identification testimony given by witnesses who saw him at the auditorium lineup on the ground that the admission of this evidence would violate his Fifth Amendment privilege against self-incrimination and Sixth Amendment right to counsel. It is well-established now that the Fourteenth Amendment makes both the Self Incrimination Clause of the Fifth Amendment and the Right to Counsel Clause of the Sixth Amendment obligatory on the States. See, *e. g., Malloy* v. *Hogan,* 378 U. S. 1; *Gideon* v. *Wainwright,* 372 U. S. 335.

I.

(a) Relying on *Schmerber* v. *California,* 384 U. S. 757, the Court rejects Gilbert's Fifth Amendment contention as to both the handwriting exemplars and the lineup identification. I dissent from that holding. For reasons set out in my separate opinion in *United State* v. *Wade, ante,* at 243, as well as in my dissent to *Schmerber,* 384 U. S., at 773, I think that case wholly unjustifiably detracts from the protection against compelled self-incrimination the Fifth Amendment was designed to afford. It rests on the ground that compelling a 'suspect to submit to or engage in conduct the sole purpose of which is to supply evidence. against himself nonetheless does not compel him to be a witness against himself. Compelling a suspect or an accused to be "the source of 'real or physical evidence' . . . ," so says *Schmerber*, 384 U. S., at 764, is not compelling him to be a witness against himself. Such an artificial distinction between things that are in reality the same is in my judgment wholly out of·line with the liberal construction which should always be given to the Bill of Rights. See *Boyd* v. *United States*, 116 U. S. 616.

(b) The Court rejects Gilbert's right-to-counsel contention in connection with the handwriting exemplars on the ground that the taking of the exemplars "was not a 'critical' stage of the criminal proceedings entitling petitioner to the assistance of counsel." In all reality, however, it was one of the most "critical" stages of the government proceedings that ended in Gilbert's conviction. As to both the State's case and Gilbert's defense, the handwriting exemplars were just as important as the lineup and perhaps more so, for handwriting analysis, being, as the Court notes, "scientific" and "systematized," *United States* v. *Wade, ante,* at 227, may carry much more weight with the jury than any kind of lineup identification. The Court, however, suggests that absence of counsel when handwriting exemplars are obtained will not impair the right of cross-examination at trial. But just as nothing said in our previous opinions "links the right to counsel only to protection of Fifth Amendment rights," *United States* v. *Wade, ante,* at 226, nothing has been said which justifies linking the right to counsel only to the protection of other Sixth Amendment rights. And there is nothing in the Constitution to justify considering the right to counsel as a second-

class, subsidiary right which attaches only when the
Court deems other specific rights in jeopardy. The real
basis for the Court's holding that the stage of obtaining
handwriting exemplars is not "critical," is its statement
that "there is minimal risk that the absence of counsel
might derogate his right to a fair trial." The Court
considers the "right to a fair trial" to be the overriding
"aim of the right to counsel," *United States* v. *Wade,
ante,* at 226, and somehow believes that this Court has
the power to balance away the constitutional guarantee
of right to counsel when the Court believes it unnecessary
to provide what the Court considers a "fair trial." But
I think this Court lacks constitutional power thus to
balance away a defendant's absolute right to counsel
which the Sixth and Fourteenth Amendments guarantee
him. The Framers did not declare in the Sixth Amendment that a defendant is entitled to a "fair trial," nor
that he is entitled to counsel on the condition that this
Court thinks there is more than· a "minimal risk" that
without a lawyer his trial will be "unfair." The Sixth
Amendment settled that a trial without a lawyer is constitutionally unfair, unless the court-created balancing
formula has somehow changed it. *Johnson* v. *Zerbst,*
304 U. S. 458, and *Gideon* v. *Wainwright,* 372 U. S. 335,
I thought finally established the right of an accused to
counsel without balancing of any kind.

The Court's holding here illustrates the danger to Bill
of Rights guarantees in the use of words like a "fair
trial" to take the place of the clearly specified safeguards
of the Constitution. I think it far safer for constitutional
rights for this Court to adhere to constitutional language
like "the accused shall . . . have the Assistance of Counsel
for his defence" instead of substituting the words not
mentioned, "the accused shall have the assistance of
counsel only if the Supreme Court thinks it necessary
to assure a fair trial." In my judgment the guarantees

of the Constitution with its Bill of Rights provide the kind of "fair trial" the Framers sought to protect. Gilbert was entitled to have the "assistance of counsel" when he was forced to supply evidence for the Government to use against him at his trial. I would reverse the case for this reason also.

II.

I agree with the Court that Gilbert's case should not be reversed for state error in admitting the pretrial statement of an accomplice which referred to Gilbert. But instead of squarely rejecting petitioner's reliance on the dissent in *Delli Paoli* v. *United States,* 352 U. S. 232, 246, the Court avoids the issue by pointing to the fact that the California Supreme Court, even assuming the error to be a federal constitutional one, applied a harmless-error test which measures up to the one we subsequently enunciated in *Chapman* v. *California,* 386 U. S. 18. And the Court then goes on to suggest that the California Supreme Court may desire to reconsider whether that is so upon remand.

I think the Court should clearly indicate that neither *Delli Paoli* nor *Chapman* has any relevance here. *Delli Paoli* rested on the admissibility of evidence in federal, not state, courts. The introduction of evidence in state courts is exclusively governed by state law unless its introduction would violate some federal constitutional provision and there is no such federal provision here. See *Spencer* v. *Texas,* 385 U. S. 554. That being so, any error in admitting the accomplice's pretrial statement is only an error of state law, and *Chapman,* providing a federal constitutional harmless-error rule, has absolutely no relevance here. Instead of looking at the harmless-error test applied by the California Supreme Court in order to ascertain whether it comports with *Chapman,* I would make it clear that this Court is leaving to the

States their unbridled power to control their own state courts in the absence of conflicting federal constitutional provisions.

III.

One witness who identified Gilbert at the guilt stage of his trial and eight witnesses who identified him at the penalty stage testified on direct examination that they had identified him in the auditorium lineup. I agree with the Court that the admission of this testimony was constitutional error and that Gilbert is entitled to a new trial unless the state courts, applying *Chapman,* conclude that this error was harmless. However, these witnesses also identified Gilbert in the courtroom and two other witnesses at the guilt stage identified him solely in the courtroom. As to these, the Court holds that "[t]he admission of the in-court identifications without first determining that they were not tainted by the illegal lineup . . . was constitutional error." I dissent from this holding in this case and in *United States* v. *Wade, ante,* at 243, for the reasons there given.

For the reasons here stated, I would vacate the judgment of the California Supreme Court and remand for consideration of whether the admission of the handwriting exemplars and the out-of-court lineup identification was harmless error.*

MR. JUSTICE DOUGLAS, concurring in part and dissenting in part.

While I agree with the Court's opinion except for Part I,† I would reverse and remand for a new trial on

---

*The Court dismisses as improvidently granted the Fourth Amendment search-and-seizure question raised by Gilbert in this case. I dissent from this, because I would decide that question against Gilbert. However, since the Court refuses to decide that question, I see no reason for expressing my views at length.

† On that phase of the case I agree with MR. JUSTICE BLACK and MR. JUSTICE FORTAS.

the search and seizure point. The search of the petitioner's home is sought to be justified by the doctrine of "hot pursuit," even though the officers conducting the search knew that petitioner, the suspected criminal, was not at home.

At about 10:30 a. m. on January 3, a California bank was robbed by two armed men; a police officer was killed by one of the robbers. Another officer shot one of the robbers, Weaver, who was captured a few blocks from the scene of the crime. Weaver told the police that he had participated in the robbery and that a person known to him as "Skinny" Gilbert was his accomplice. He told the officers that Gilbert lived in Apartment 28 of "a Hawaiian sounding named apartment house" on Los Feliz Boulevard. This information was given to the Federal Bureau of Investigation and was broadcast to a field agent, Kiel, who was instructed to find the apartment. Kiel located the "Lanai," an apartment on Los Feliz Boulevard, at about 1 p. m., informed the radio control, and engaged the apartment manager in conversation. While they were talking, a man gave a key to the manager and told her that he was going to San Francisco for a few days. Agent Kiel learned from the manager that Flood, one of the two men who had rented Apartment 28 the previous day, was the man who had just turned in the key and left by the rear exit. The agent ran out into the alleyway but saw no one.

In the meantime, the federal officers learned from Weaver that Gilbert was registered under the name of Flood. They also learned that three men may have been involved in the robbery—the two who entered the bank and a third driving the getaway car. About 1:10 p. m., additional federal agents arrived at the apartment, in response to Agent Kiel's radio summons. Kiel told them that the resident of Apartment 28 was a Robert Flood who had just left. The agents obtained a key from the manager, entered the apartment and searched for a person or a hiding place for a person. They found no one. But they did find an envelope containing pictures of petitioner; the pictures were seized and shown to bank employees for identification. The agents also found a notebook containing a diagram of the area surrounding the bank, a clip from an automatic pistol, and a bag containing rolls of coins bearing the marking of the robbed bank. On the basis of this information, a search warrant was issued, and the automatic clip, notebook, and coin rolls were seized. Petitioner was arrested in Pennsylvania on February 26. The evidence seized during the search of his apartment was introduced in evidence at his trial for murder.

The California Supreme Court justified the search on the ground that the police were in hot pursuit of the suspected bank robbers. The entry of the apartment was lawful. The subsequent search and seizure were lawful since the officers were trying to further identify suspects and to facilitate continued pursuit. 63 Cal. 2d 690, 408 P. 2d 365.

I have set forth the testimony relating to the search more fully in the Appendix to this opinion. For the reasons stated there, I cannot agree that "the facts do not appear with sufficient clarity to enable us to decide" the serious question presented.

Since the search and seizure took place without a warrant, it can stand only if it comes within one of the narrowly defined exceptions to the rule that a search and seizure must rest upon a validly executed search warrant. See, *e. g., United States* v. *Jeffers,* 342 U. S. 48, 51; *Jones* v. *United States,* 357 U. S. 493; *Rios* v. *United States,* 364 U. S. 253, 261; *Stoner* v. *California,* 376 U. S. 483, 486. One of these exceptions is that officers having probable cause to arrest may enter a dwelling to make the arrest and conduct a contemporaneous search of the place of arrest "in order to find and seize things connected with the crime as its fruits or as the means by which it was committed, as well as weapons and other things to effect an escape from custody." *Agnello* v. *United States,* 269 U. S. 20, 30. This, of course, assumes that an arrest has been made, and that the search "is substantially contemporaneous with the arrest and is confined to the immediate vicinity of the arrest." *Stoner* v. *California, supra,* at 486. In this case, the exemption is not applicable since the arrest was made many days after the search and at a location far removed from the search.

Here, the officers entered the apartment, searched for petitioner and did not find him. Nevertheless, they continued searching the apartment and seized the pictures; the inescapable conclusion is that they were searching for evidence linking petitioner to the bank robbery, not for the suspected robbers. The court below said that, having legally entered the apartment, the officers "could properly look through the apartment for anything that could be used to identify the suspects or to expedite the pursuit." 63 Cal. 2d, at 707, 408 P. 2d, at 375.

Prior to this case, police could enter and search a house without a warrant only incidental to a valid arrest. If this judgment stands, the police can search a house for evidence, even though the suspect is not arrested. The purpose of the search is, in the words of the California Supreme Court, "limited to and incident to the purpose of the officers' entry"—that is, to apprehend the suspected criminal. Under that doctrine, the police are given license to search for any evidence linking the homeowner with the crime. Certainly such evidence is well calculated "to identify the suspects," and will "expedite the pursuit" since the police can then concentrate on the person whose home has been ransacked. *Ibid.*

The search and seizure in this case violates another limitation, which concededly the ill-starred decision in *Harris* v. *United States,* 331 U. S. 145, flouted, *viz.,* that a general search for evidence, even when the police are in "hot pursuit" or have a warrant of arrest, does not make constitutional a general search of a room or of a house (*United States* v. *Lefkowitz,* 285 U. S. 452, 463–464). If it did, then the police, acting without a search warrant, could search more extensively than when they have a warrant. For the warrant must, as prescribed by the Fourth Amendment, "particularly" describe the "things to be seized." As stated by the Court in *United States* v. *Lefkowitz, supra,* p. 464:

> "The authority of officers to search one's house or place of business contemporaneously with his lawful arrest therein upon a valid warrant of arrest certainly is not greater than that conferred by a search warrant issued upon adequate proof and sufficiently describing the premises and the things sought to be obtained. Indeed, the informed and deliberate determinations of magistrates empowered to issue warrants as to what searches and seizures are permissible under the Constitution are to be preferred over the hurried action of officers and others who may happen to make arrests. Security against unlawful searches is more likely to be attained by resort to search warrants than by reliance upon the caution and sagacity of petty officers while acting under the excitement that attends the capture of persons accused of crime."

Indeed, if at the very start, there had been a search warrant authorizing the seizure of the automatic clip, notebook, and coin rolls, the envelope containing pictures of petitioner could not have been seized. "The requirement that warrants shall particularly describe the things to be seized . . . prevents the seizure of one thing under a warrant describing another. As to what is to be taken, nothing is left to the discretion of the officer executing the warrant." *Marron* v. *United States,* 275 U. S. 192, 196.

The modern police technique of ransacking houses, even to the point of seizing their entire contents as was done in *Kremen* v. *United States,* 353 U. S. 346, is a shocking departure from the philosophy of the Fourth Amendment. For the kind of search conducted here was indeed a general search. And if the Fourth Amendment was aimed at any particular target it was aimed at that. When we take that step, we resurrect one of the deepest-rooted complaints that gave rise to our Revolution. As the Court stated in *Boyd* v. *United States,* 116 U. S. 616, 625:

> "The practice had obtained in the colonies of issuing writs of assistance to the revenue officers, empowering them, in their discretion, to search suspected places for smuggled goods, which James Otis pronounced 'the worst instrument of arbitrary power, the most destructive of English liberty, and the fundamental principles of law, that ever was found in an English law book'; since they placed 'the liberty of every man in the hands of every petty officer.' This was in February, 1761, in Boston, and the famous debate in which it occurred was perhaps the most prominent event which inaugurated the resistance of the colonies to the oppressions of the mother country. 'Then and there,' said John Adams, 'then and there was the first scene of the first act of opposition to the arbitrary claims of Great Britain. Then and there the child Independence was born.'"

I would not allow the general search to reappear on the American scene.

APPENDIX TO OPINION OF
MR. JUSTICE DOUGLAS.

As the Court notes, there is some confusion in the record respecting the timing of events surrounding the search and the breadth of purpose with which the search was conducted. The confusion results from the testimony of the agents involved.

Agent Kiel testified that Agents Schlatter and Onsgaard arrived at the apartment at about 1:10 and entered the apartment a minute or two after their arrival. Kiel received the photographs from Agent Schlatter between 1:25 and 1:30.

Agent Schlatter testified that he, Agent Onsgaard and some local police arrived at the apartment about 1:05 and that Agent Crowley and one or two local police officers arrived in another car at the same time. Schlatter briefly talked to Kiel and the apartment manager and then entered the apartment. Upon entering he saw no one. He "made a very fast search of the apartment for a person or a hiding place of a person and . . . found none." This search took "a matter of seconds or a minute at the outside" and "[a]fter we had searched for [a] person or persons, and no one was there, it then became a matter of a stake-out under the assumption that the person or persons involved would come back." It seemed to Schlatter that "an agent had [the photograph] in his hand," when he first saw it, that it "was in the hands of an agent or an officer," and Schlatter had "a vague recollection that [the agent or officer told him he had found it] in the bedroom . . . ." There were a number of photographs. Schlatter took the photographs out to Kiel and instructed him to take one of them to the savings and loan and see if anyone there could recognize the photograph. Schlatter testified that he was in the apartment for about 30 minutes after making the search and left other agents behind when he left.

Agent Crowley testified that he entered the apartment "around 1:30, give or take a few minutes either way" and that he would say that the other officers had been in the apartment less than five minutes before he entered. He believed that "the officers and the other agent who had been with [him] at the rear of the building when the first entry was made, entered with [him]." When Crowley entered the apartment it "had already been searched for people." He received "instructions . . . to look through the apartment for anything we could find that we could use to identify or continue the pursuit of this person without conducting a detailed search." In the bedroom, on the dresser, Crowley saw an envelope bearing the name "Marlboro Photo Studio"; it appeared to him to be an envelope containing photos and he could see that there was something inside. Crowley opened the envelope and saw several copies of photographs. He discussed the matter with "Onsgaard who was in charge in the building and he instructed [Crowley] to give it to another agent for him to utilize in pursuing the investigation, and [he was] reasonably certain that that agent was Mr. Schlatter." This was about 1:30 according to Crowley. In the course of his search which turned up the photographs, Crowley "turned over [items] to see what was on the reverse, such as business cards, sales slips from local stores, that sort of item which might have been folded and would appear to possibly contain information of value to pursuit." He relayed the information obtained in this manner to the man coordinating the operation. Crowley remained in the apartment until the next morning.

Agent Townsend testified that he arrived at the apartment "[s]ometime between perhaps 1:30 and 2:00." Within an hour of his arrival, he began a search. Townsend testified that he, Agent Crowley, another agent and a local officer "looked through the bedroom closet and

GILBERT v. CALIFORNIA.

the dresser and I think the headstand." This was after
it was known that no one, other than agents and police
officers, was in the apartment. Townsend stated that
the agents and officers were "[i]n and out of the bedroom," that he found money in the bedroom dresser
about an hour after he arrived in the apartment, and
that he could not "say specifically" whether Crowley was
there at that time.

Thus, there is some conflict regarding the times at
which the events took place and with respect to the
nature of the searches conducted by the various officers.
The way I read the record, however, it is not in such a
state "that the facts do not appear with sufficient clarity
to enable us to decide" the question presented. Crowley's
testimony that he came upon the photographs while
searching "for anything . . . that we could use to identify
or continue the pursuit" stands uncontradicted, as does
his testimony that the apartment had already been
searched for a person prior to his search uncovering the
photographs. Schlatter's testimony that the operation
"became a matter of a stake-out" after the unsuccessful
search for a person does not contradict Crowley's testimony. A search for identifying evidence is certainly
compatible with a "stake-out." And Crowley best knew
what he was doing when he discovered the photographs.
Nor does Townsend's testimony that he and others, perhaps including Crowley, conducted a detailed search conflict with Crowley's testimony. First, the record indicates
that the detailed search was conducted after the photographs had been found. According to the testimony of
Kiel and Schlatter, Schlatter gave the photographs to
Kiel at about 1:30; according to Townsend, he arrived
sometime between 1:30 and 2. Second, even if the
detailed search took place before Crowley found the
photographs and Crowley participated in that search,
that does not indicate that Crowley's search which turned

up the photographs was more limited than Crowley claimed. If anything, it would indicate that his search was more general than he stated. Finally, Townsend's testimony as to the general search does not conflict with Schlatter's testimony that the operation became a "stake-out" after the suspect was not found. As I have said, a "stake-out" does not preclude a detailed search for evidence. And, the record indicates that Schlatter was not in the apartment when Townsend and the others conducted the detailed search.

The way I read the record, the photographs were discovered in the course of a general search for evidence. But even if Crowley is not believed and his testimony relating to the nature of his search is thrown out and it is simply assumed that he came upon the envelope in the course of a search for the suspect, there was no reason to pry into the envelope and seize the pictures—other than to obtain evidence. An envelope would contain neither the suspect nor the weapon.

MR. JUSTICE WHITE, whom MR. JUSTICE HARLAN and MR. JUSTICE STEWART join, concurring in part and dissenting in part.

I concur in Parts I, II, and III of the Court's opinion, but for the reasons stated in my dissenting opinion in *United States* v. *Wade, ante,* p. 250, I dissent from Part IV of the Court's opinion and would therefore affirm the judgment of the Supreme Court of California.

MR. JUSTICE FORTAS, with whom THE CHIEF JUSTICE joins, concurring in part and dissenting in part.

I concur in the result—the vacation of the judgment of the California Supreme Court and the remand of the case—but I do not believe that it is adequate. I would reverse and remand for a new trial on the additional ground that petitioner was entitled by the Sixth and

Fourteenth Amendments to be advised that he had a
right to counsel before and in connection with his
response to the prosecutor's demand for a handwriting
exemplar.

1. The giving of the handwriting exemplar is a "critical stage" of the proceeding, as my Brother Black states.
It is a "critical stage" as much as is a lineup. See *United
States* v. *Wade, ante,* p. 218. Depending upon circumstances, both may be inoffensive to the Constitution,
totally fair to the accused, and entirely reliable for the
administration of justice. On the other hand, each may
be constitutionally offensive, totally unfair to the accused,
and prejudicial to the ascertainment of truth. An accused
whose handwriting exemplar is sought needs counsel: Is
he to write "Your money or your life?" Is he to emulate
the holdup note by using red ink, brown paper, large
letters, etc.? Is the demanded handwriting exemplar, in
effect, an inculpation—a confession? Cf. the eloquent
arguments as to the need for counsel, in the Court's
opinion in *United States* v. *Wade, supra.*

2. The Court today appears to hold that an accused
may be compelled to give a handwriting exemplar. Cf.
Schmerber v. *California,* 384 U. S. 757 (1966). Presumably, he may be punished if he adamantly refuses. Unlike blood, handwriting cannot be extracted by a doctor
from an accused's veins while the accused is subjected to
physical restraint, which *Schmerber* permits. So presumably, on the basis of the Court's decision, trial courts
may hold an accused in contempt and keep him in jail—
indefinitely—until he gives a handwriting exemplar.

This decision goes beyond *Schmerber.* Here the accused, in the absence of any warning that he has a right
to counsel, is compelled to cooperate, not merely to submit; to engage in a volitional act, not merely to suffer
the inevitable consequences of arrest and state custody;
to take affirmative action which may not merely identify

him, but tie him directly to the crime. I dissented in
Schmerber. For reasons stated in my dissent in *United
States* v. *Wade, supra,* I regard the extension of *Schmer-
ber* as impermissible.

In *Wade,* the accused, who is compelled to utter the
words used by the criminal in the heat of his act, has at
least the comfort of counsel—even if the Court denies
that the accused may refuse to speak the words—because
the compelled utterance occurs in the course of a lineup.
In the present case, the Court deprives him of even this
source of comfort and whatever protection counsel's
ingenuity could provide in face of the Court's opinion.
This is utterly insupportable, in my respectful opinion.
This is not like fingerprinting, measuring, photographing—or even blood-taking. It is a process involving the
use of discretion. It is capable of abuse. It is in the
stream of inculpation. Cross-examination can play only
a limited role in offsetting false inference or misleading
coincidence from a "stacked" handwriting exemplar.
The Court's reference to the efficacy of cross-examination
in this situation is much more of a comfort to an appellate court than a source of solace to the defendant and
his counsel.

3. I agree with the Court's condemnation of the
lineup identifications here and the consequent in-court
identifications, and I join in this part of its opinion. I
would also reverse and remand for a new trial because
of the use of the handwriting exemplar which was unconstitutionally obtained in the absence of advice to the
accused as to the availability of counsel. I could not
conclude that the violation of the privilege against self-
incrimination implicit in the facts relating to the exemplar was waived in the absence of advice as to counsel.
In re Gault, 387 U. S. 1, 41–42 (1967); *Miranda* v. *Arizona,* 384 U. S. 436 (1966).

STOVALL *v.* DENNO.

STOVALL *v.* DENNO, WARDEN.

CERTIORARI TO THE UNITED STATES COURT OF APPEALS FOR
THE SECOND CIRCUIT.

No. 254.   Argued February 16, 1967.—Decided June 12, 1967.

Petitioner was convicted and sentenced to death for murdering one
Dr. Behrendt. He had been arrested the day after the murder and
without being afforded time to retain counsel was taken by police
officers, to one of whom he was handcuffed, to be viewed at the
hospital by Mrs. Behrendt, who had been seriously wounded by
her husband's assailant. After observing him and hearing him
speak as directed by an officer, Mrs. Behrendt identified petitioner
as the murderer. Mrs. Behrendt and the officers testified at petitioner's trial as to the hospital identification and she also made an
in-court identification of the petitioner. Following affirmance of
his conviction by the highest state court, petitioner sought habeas
corpus in the District Court claiming that Mrs. Behrendt's identification testimony violated his Fifth, Sixth, and Fourteenth Amendment rights. The District Court after hearing argument on an
unrelated claim dismissed the petition. The Court of Appeals,
en banc, vacated a panel decision reversing the dismissal of the
petition on constitutional grounds, and affirmed the District Court.
Held:

   1. The constitutional rule established in today's decisions in
United States v. *Wade* and *Gilbert* v. *California, ante,* pp. 218, 263,
has application only to cases involving confrontations for identification purposes conducted in the absence of counsel after this
date. Cf. *Linkletter* v. *Walker,* 381 U. S. 618; *Tehan* v. *Shott,*
382 U. S. 406; *Johnson* v. *New Jersey,* 384 U. S. 719.   Pp. 296–301.

   2. Though the practice of showing suspects singly for purposes
of identification has been widely condemned, a violation of due
process of law in the conduct of a confrontation depends on the
totality of the surrounding circumstances. There was no due
process denial in the confrontation here since Mrs. Behrendt was
the only person who could exonerate the suspect; she could not
go to the police station for the usual lineup; and there was no
way of knowing how long she would live.   Pp. 301–302.

355 F. 2d 731, affirmed.

Leon B. Polsky argued the cause and filed briefs for petitioner.

William Cahn argued the cause and filed a brief for respondent.

H. Richard Uviller argued the cause and filed a brief for the New York State District Attorneys' Association, as *amicus curiae*, urging affirmance.

Louis J. Lefkowitz, Attorney General, *pro se, Samuel A. Hirshowitz*, First Assistant Attorney General, and *Barry Mahoney*, Assistant Attorney General, filed a brief for the Attorney General of New York, as *amicus curiae*, urging affirmance.

MR. JUSTICE BRENNAN delivered the opinion of the Court.

This federal habeas corpus proceeding attacks collaterally a state criminal conviction for the same alleged constitutional errors in the admission of allegedly tainted identification evidence that were before us on direct review of the convictions involved in *United States* v. *Wade, ante,* p. 218, and *Gilbert* v. *California, ante,* p. 263. This case therefore provides a vehicle for deciding the extent to which the rules announced in *Wade* and *Gilbert*— requiring the exclusion of identification evidence which is tainted by exhibiting the accused to identifying witnesses before trial in the absence of his counsel—are to be applied retroactively. See *Linkletter* v. *Walker,* 381 U. S. 618; *Tehan* v. *Shott,* 382 U. S. 406; *Johnson* v. *New Jersey,* 384 U. S. 719.[1] A further question is whether in any event, on the facts of the particular con-

---

[1] Although respondent did not raise the bar of retroactivity, the Attorney General of the State of New York, as *amicus curiae*, extensively briefed the issue of retroactivity and petitioner, in his reply brief, addressed himself to this question. Compare *Mapp* v. *Ohio,* 367 U. S. 643, 646, n. 3.

frontation involved in this case, petitioner was denied due process of law in violation of the Fourteenth Amendment. Cf. *Davis* v. *North Carolina,* 384 U. S. 737.

Dr. Paul Behrendt was stabbed to death in the kitchen of his home in Garden City, Long Island, about midnight August 23, 1961. Dr. Behrendt's wife, also a physician, had followed her husband to the kitchen and jumped at the assailant. He knocked her to the floor and stabbed her 11 times. The police found a shirt on the kitchen floor and keys in a pocket which they traced to petitioner. They arrested him on the afternoon of August 24. An arraignment was promptly held but was postponed until petitioner could retain counsel.

Mrs. Behrendt was hospitalized for major surgery to save her life. The police, without affording petitioner time to retain counsel, arranged with her surgeon to permit them to bring petitioner to her hospital room about noon of August 25, the day after the surgery. Petitioner was handcuffed to one of five police officers who, with two members of the staff of the District Attorney, brought him to the hospital room. Petitioner was the only Negro in the room. Mrs. Behrendt identified him from her hospital bed after being asked by an officer whether he "was the man" and after petitioner repeated at the direction of an officer a "few words for voice identification." None of the witnesses could recall the words that were used. Mrs. Behrendt and the officers testified at the trial to her identification of the petitioner in the hospital room, and she also made an in-court identification of petitioner in the courtroom.

Petitioner was convicted and sentenced to death. The New York Court of Appeals affirmed without opinion. 13 N. Y. 2d 1094, 196 N. E. 2d 65. Petitioner *pro se* sought federal habeas corpus in the District Court for the Southern District of New York. He claimed that among other constitutional rights allegedly denied him at his trial, the admission of Mrs. Behrendt's identification testimony violated his rights under the Fifth, Sixth, and Fourteenth Amendments because he had been compelled to submit to the hospital room confrontation without the help of counsel and under circumstances which unfairly focussed the witness' attention on him as the man believed by the police to be the guilty person. The District Court dismissed the petition after hearing argument on an unrelated claim of an alleged invalid search and seizure. On appeal to the Court of Appeals for the Second Circuit a panel of that court initially reversed the dismissal after reaching the issue of the admissibility of Mrs. Behrendt's identification evidence and holding it inadmissible on the ground that the hospital room identification violated petitioner's constitutional right to the assistance of counsel. The Court of Appeals thereafter heard the case *en banc,* vacated the panel decision, and affirmed the District Court. 355 F. 2d 731. We granted certiorari, 384 U. S. 1000, and set the case for argument with *Wade* and *Gilbert.* We hold that *Wade* and *Gilbert* affect only those cases and all future cases which involve confrontations for identification purposes conducted in the absence of counsel after this date. The rulings of *Wade* and *Gilbert* are therefore inapplicable in the present case. We think also that on the facts of this case petitioner was not deprived of due process of law in violation of the Fourteenth Amendment. The judgment of the Court of Appeals is, therefore, affirmed.

I.

Our recent discussions of the retroactivity of other constitutional rules of criminal procedure make unnecessary any detailed treatment of that question here. *Linkletter* v. *Walker, supra; Tehan* v. *Shott, supra; Johnson* v. *New Jersey, supra.* "These cases establish the principle that in criminal litigation concerning constitutional

STOVALL v. DENNO.

claims, 'the Court may in the interest of justice make the rule prospective . . . where the exigencies of the situation require such an application'. . . ." *Johnson, supra,* 384 U. S., at 726–727. The criteria guiding resolution of the question implicate (a) the purpose to be served by the new standards, (b) the extent of the reliance by law enforcement authorities on the old standards, and (c) the effect on the administration of justice of a retroactive application of the new standards. "[T]he retroactivity or nonretroactivity of a rule is not automatically determined by the provision of the Constitution on which the dictate is based. Each constitutional rule of criminal procedure has its own distinct functions, its own background of precedent, and its own impact on the administration of justice, and the way in which these factors combine must inevitably vary with the dictate involved." *Johnson, supra,* at 728.

Wade and *Gilbert* fashion exclusionary rules to deter law enforcement authorities from exhibiting an accused to witnesses before trial for identification purposes without notice to and in the absence of counsel. A conviction which rests on a mistaken identification is a gross miscarriage of justice. The *Wade* and *Gilbert* rules are aimed at minimizing that possibility by preventing the unfairness at the pretrial confrontation that experience has proved can occur and assuring meaningful examination of the identification witness' testimony at trial. Does it follow that the rules should be applied retroactively? We do not think so.

It is true that the right to the assistance of counsel has been applied retroactively at stages of the prosecution where denial of the right must almost invariably deny a fair trial, for example, at the trial itself, *Gideon* v. *Wainwright,* 372 U. S. 335, or at some forms of arraignment, *Hamilton* v. *Alabama,* 368 U. S. 52, or on appeal, *Douglas* v. *California,* 372 U. S. 353. "The basic purpose of a trial is the determination of truth, and it is self-evident that to deny a lawyer's help through the technical intricacies of a criminal trial or to deny a full opportunity to appeal a conviction because the accused is poor is to impede that purpose and to infect a criminal proceeding with the clear danger of convicting the innocent." *Tehan* v. *Shott, supra,* at 416. We have also retroactively applied rules of criminal procedure fashioned to correct serious flaws in the fact-finding process at trial. See for example *Jackson* v. *Denno,* 378 U. S. 368. Although the *Wade* and *Gilbert* rules also are aimed at avoiding unfairness at the trial by enhancing the reliability of the fact-finding process in the area of identification evidence, "the question whether a constitutional rule of criminal procedure does or does not enhance the reliability of the fact-finding process at trial is necessarily a matter of degree." *Johnson* v. *New Jersey, supra,* at 728–729. The extent to which a condemned practice infects the integrity of the truth-determining process at trial is a "question of probabilities." 384 U. S., at 729. Such probabilities must in turn be weighed against the prior justified reliance upon the old standard and the impact of retroactivity upon the administration of justice.

We have outlined in *Wade* the dangers and unfairness inherent in confrontations for identification. The possibility of unfairness at that point is great, both because of the manner in which confrontations are frequently conducted, and because of the likelihood that the accused will often be precluded from reconstructing what occurred and thereby from obtaining a full hearing on the identification issue at trial. The presence of counsel will significantly promote fairness at the confrontation and a full hearing at trial on the issue of identification. We have, therefore, concluded that the confrontation is a "critical stage," and that counsel is required at all confrontations. It must be recognized, however, that, unlike

196

cases in which counsel is absent at trial or on appeal, it may confidently be assumed that confrontations for identification can be and often have been conducted in the absence of counsel with scrupulous fairness and without prejudice to the accused at trial. Therefore, while we feel that the exclusionary rules set forth in *Wade* and *Gilbert* are justified by the need to assure the integrity and reliability of our system of justice, they undoubtedly will affect cases in which no unfairness will be present. Of course, we should also assume there have been injustices in the past which could have been averted by having counsel present at the confrontation for identification, just as there are injustices when counsel is absent at trial. But the certainty and frequency with which we can say in the confrontation cases that no injustice occurred differs greatly enough from the cases involving absence of counsel at trial or on appeal to justify treating the situations as different in kind for the purpose of retroactive application, especially in light of the strong countervailing interests outlined below, and because it remains open to all persons to allege and prove, as Stovall attempts to do in this case, that the confrontation resulted in such unfairness that it infringed his right to due process of law. See *Palmer* v. *Peyton*, 359 F. 2d 199 (C. A. 4th Cir. 1966).

The unusual force of the countervailing considerations strengthens our conclusion in favor of prospective application. The law enforcement officials of the Federal Government and of all 50 States have heretofore proceeded on the premise that the Constitution did not require the presence of counsel at pretrial confrontations for identification. Today's rulings were not foreshadowed in our cases; no court announced such a requirement until *Wade* was decided by the Court of Appeals for the Fifth Circuit, 358 F. 2d 557. The overwhelming majority of American courts have always treated the evidence ques-

tion not as one of admissibility but as one of credibility
for the jury. Wall, Eye-Witness Identification in Criminal Cases 38. Law enforcement authorities fairly relied
on this virtually unanimous weight of authority, now no
longer valid, in conducting pretrial confrontations in
the absence of counsel. It is, therefore, very clear that
retroactive application of *Wade* and *Gilbert* "would seriously disrupt the administration of our criminal laws."
Johnson v. *New Jersey, supra,* at 731. In *Tehan* v.
Shott, supra, we thought it persuasive against retroactive application of the no-comment rule of *Griffin* v.
California, 380 U. S. 609, that such application would
have a serious impact on the six States that allowed
comment on an accused's failure to take the stand. We
said, "To require all of those States now to void the
conviction of every person who did not testify at his
trial would have an impact upon the administration of
their criminal law so devastating as to need no elaboration." 382 U. S., at 419. That impact is insignificant
compared to the impact to be expected from retroactivity
of the *Wade* and *Gilbert* rules. At the very least, the
processing of current criminal calendars would be dis-
rupted while hearings were conducted to determine taint,
if any, in identification evidence, and whether in any
event the admission of the evidence was harmless error.
Doubtless, too, inquiry would be handicapped by the
unavailability of witnesses and dim memories. We conclude, therefore, that the *Wade* and *Gilbert* rules should
not be made retroactive.

We also conclude that, for these purposes, no distinction is justified between convictions now final, as in the
instant case, and convictions at various stages of trial and
direct review. We regard the factors of reliance and
burden on the administration of justice as entitled to
such overriding significance as to make that distinction

unsupportable.[2] We recognize that Wade and Gilbert are, therefore, the only victims of pretrial confrontations in the absence of their counsel to have the benefit of the rules established in their cases. That they must be given that benefit is, however, an unavoidable consequence of the necessity that constitutional adjudications not stand as mere dictum. Sound policies of decision-making, rooted in the command of Article III of the Constitution that we resolve issues solely in concrete cases or controversies,[3] and in the possible effect upon the incentive of counsel to advance contentions requiring a change in the law,[4] militate against denying Wade and Gilbert the benefit of today's decisions. Inequity arguably results from according the benefit of a new rule to the parties in the case in which it is announced but not to other litigants similarly situated in the trial or appellate process who have raised the same issue.[5] But we regard the fact that the parties involved are chance beneficiaries as an insignificant cost for adherence to sound principles of decision-making.

II.

We turn now to the question whether petitioner, although not entitled to the application of *Wade* and *Gilbert* to his case, is entitled to relief on his claim that in any event the confrontation conducted in this

[2] Schaefer, The Control of "Sunbursts": Techniques of Prospective Overruling, 22 Record of N. Y. C. B. A. 394, 408–411 (1967).

[3] Note, Prospective Overruling and Retroactive Application in the Federal Courts, 71 Yale L. J. 907, 930–933 (1962).

[4] See Mishkin, Foreword, The Supreme Court 1964 Term, 79 Harv. L. Rev. 56, 60–61 (1965).

[5] See Mishkin, n. 4, *supra,* at 61, n. 23; Bender, The Retroactive Effect of an Overruling Constitutional Decision: *Mapp* v. *Ohio,* 110 U. Pa. L. Rev. 650, 675–678 (1962); Schwartz, Retroactivity, Reliability, and Due Process: A Reply to Professor Mishkin, 33 U. Chi. L. Rev. 719, 764 (1966).

case was so unnecessarily suggestive and conducive to irreparable mistaken identification that he was denied due process of law. This is a recognized ground of attack upon a conviction independent of any right to counsel claim. *Palmer* v. *Peyton*, 359 F. 2d 199 (C. A. 4th Cir. 1966). The practice of showing suspects singly to persons for the purpose of identification, and not as part of a lineup, has been widely condemned.[6] However, a claimed violation of due process of law in the conduct of a confrontation depends on the totality of the circumstances surrounding it, and the record in the present case reveals that the showing of Stovall to Mrs. Behrendt in an immediate hospital confrontation was imperative. The Court of Appeals, *en banc*, stated, 355 F. 2d, at 735,

> "Here was the only person in the world who could possibly exonerate Stovall. Her words, and only her words, 'He is not the man' could have resulted in freedom for Stovall. The hospital was not far distant from the courthouse and jail. No one knew how long Mrs. Behrendt might live. Faced with the responsibility of identifying the attacker, with the need for immediate action and with the knowledge that Mrs. Behrendt could not visit the jail, the police followed the only feasible procedure and took Stovall to the hospital room. Under these circumstances, the usual police station line-up, which Stovall now argues he should have had, was out of the question."

The judgment of the Court of Appeals is affirmed.

It is so ordered.

MR. JUSTICE DOUGLAS is of the view that the deprivation of the right to counsel in the setting of this case

---

[6] See Wall, Eye-Witness Identification in Criminal Cases 26–40; Paul, Identification of Accused Persons, 12 Austl. L. J. 42, 44 (1938);

should be given retroactive effect as it was in *Gideon* v. *Wainwright*, 372 U. S. 335, and in *Douglas* v. *California*, 372 U. S. 353. And see *Linkletter* v. *Walker*, 381 U. S. 618, 640 (dissenting opinion); *Johnson* v. *New Jersey*, 384 U. S. 719, 736 (dissenting opinion).

MR. JUSTICE FORTAS would reverse and remand for a new trial on the ground that the State's reference at trial to the improper hospital identification violated petitioner's Fourteenth Amendment rights and was prejudicial. He would not reach the question of retroactivity of *Wade* and *Gilbert*.

MR. JUSTICE WHITE, whom MR. JUSTICE HARLAN and MR. JUSTICE STEWART join, concurring in the result.

For the reasons stated in my dissenting opinion in *United States* v. *Wade, ante,* p. 250, I perceive no constitutional error in the identification procedure to which the petitioner was subjected. I concur in the result and in that portion of the Court's opinion which limits application of the new Sixth Amendment rule.

MR. JUSTICE BLACK, dissenting.

In *United States* v. *Wade, ante,* p. 218, and *Gilbert* v. *California, ante,* p. 263, the Court holds that lineup identification testimony should be excluded if it was obtained by exhibiting an accused to identifying witnesses before trial in the absence of his counsel. I concurred in those holdings as to out-of-court lineup identification on the ground that the right to counsel is guaranteed in federal courts by the Sixth Amendment and in state courts by the Sixth and Fourteenth Amendments. The first question in this case is whether other defendants, already in prison on

Williams & Hammelmann, Identification Parades, Part I, [1963] Crim. L. Rev. 479, 480–481; Frankfurter, The Case of Sacco and Vanzetti 31–32.

such unconstitutional evidence, shall be accorded the benefit of the rule. In this case the Court holds that the petitioner here, convicted on such unconstitutional evidence, must remain in prison, and that besides Wade and Gilbert, who are "chance beneficiaries," no one can invoke the rule except defendants exhibited in lineups in the future. I dissent from that holding. It keeps people serving sentences who were convicted through the use of unconstitutional evidence. This is sought to be justified on the ground that retroactive application of the holding in *Gilbert* and *Wade* would somehow work a "burden on the administration of justice" and would not serve the Court's purpose "to deter law enforcement authorities." It seems to me that to deny this petitioner and others like him the benefit of the new rule deprives them of a constitutional trial and perpetrates a rank discrimination against them. Once the Court determines what the Constitution says, I do not believe it has the power, by weighing "countervailing interests," to legislate a timetable by which the Constitution's provisions shall become effective. For reasons stated in my dissent in *Linkletter* v. *Walker,* 381 U. S. 618, 640, I would hold that the petitioner here and every other person in jail under convictions based on unconstitutional evidence should be given the advantage of today's newly announced constitutional rules.

The Court goes on, however, to hold that even though its new constitutional rule about the Sixth Amendment's right to counsel cannot help this petitioner, he is nevertheless entitled to a consideration of his claim, "independent of any right to counsel claim," that his identification by one of the victims of the robbery was made under circumstances so "unfair" that he was denied "due process of law" guaranteed by the Fourteenth Amendment. Although the Court finds petitioner's claim without merit, I dissent from its holding that a general claim of "unfairness" at the lineup is "open to all persons to allege and prove." The term "due process of law" is a direct descendant of Magna Charta's promise of a trial according to the "law of the land" as it has been established by the lawmaking agency, constitutional or legislative. No one has ever been able to point to a word in our constitutional history that shows the Framers ever intended that the Due Process Clause of the Fifth or Fourteenth Amendment was designed to mean any more than that defendants charged with crimes should be entitled to a trial governed by the laws, constitutional and statutory, that are in existence at the time of the commission of the crime and the time of the trial. The concept of due process under which the Court purports to decide this question, however, is that this Court looks at "the totality of the circumstances" of a particular case to determine in its own judgment whether they comport with the Court's notion of decency, fairness, and fundamental justice, and, if so, declares they comport with the Constitution, and, if not, declares they are forbidden by the Constitution. See, *e. g., Rochin* v. *California,* 342 U. S. 165. Such a constitutional formula substitutes this Court's judgment of what is right for what the Constitution declares shall be the supreme law of the land. This due process notion proceeds as though our written Constitution, designed to grant limited powers to government, had neutralized its limitations by using the Due Process Clause to authorize this Court to override its written limiting language by substituting the Court's view of what powers the Framers should have granted government. Once again I dissent from any such view of the Constitution. Where accepted, its result is to make this Court not a Constitution-interpreter, but a day-to-day Constitution-maker.

But even if the Due Process Clause could possibly be construed as giving such latitudinal powers to the

Court, I would still think the Court goes too far in holding that the courts can look at the particular circumstances of each identification lineup to determine at large whether they are too "suggestive and conducive to irreparable mistaken identification" to be constitutional. That result is to freeze as constitutional or as unconstitutional the circumstances of each case, giving the States and the Federal Government no permanent constitutional standards. It also transfers to this Court power to determine what the Constitution should say, instead of performance of its undoubted constitutional power to determine what the Constitution does say. And the result in this particular case is to put into a constitutional mould a rule of evidence which I think is plainly within the constitutional powers of the States in creating and enforcing their own criminal laws. I must say with all deference that for this Court to hold that the Due Process Clause gives it power to bar state introduction of lineup testimony on its notion of fairness, not because it violates some specific constitutional prohibition, is an arbitrary, wholly capricious action.

I would not affirm this case but would reverse and remand for consideration of whether the out-of-court lineup identification of petitioner was, under *Chapman* v. *California,* 386 U. S. 18, harmless error. If it was not, petitioner is entitled to a new trial because of a denial of the right to counsel guaranteed by the Sixth Amendment which the Fourteenth Amendment makes obligatory on the States.

BIBLIOGRAPHY

Bertillon: "Photographic Judiciaire"

Boring, Langfeld, Weld: "Introduction to Psychology"

Encyclopedia Britannica: 14th Ed., Vols. 9,15

Sir Francis Dalton: "Finger Prints"

G.E.: Photo Data Book

J. Edgar Hoover: "Problems of Identification"

Kersta: "Voiceprints"

M.D. Medical Magazine, Vol. 11, No.8

Munn: "Psychology"

Marshall: "Law and Psychology in Conflict"

Mark Twain: "Pudd'nhead Wilson"

N.Y.C. Police Dept.: "Lineup Identification Procedure"
    (T.O.P. #318)

Richardson "Evidence"

Ringel: "Arrests, Searches and Confessions"

Sir James Stephen: "History of Criminal Law"

Schatkin: "Paternity Blood Grouping Tests"

Schatkin: "Disputed Paternity Proceedings"

Shapiro "Dictionary of Legal Terms"

Vergat: "Les Rites Secretes des Primitifs de L'Oubanqui"

Wilder and Wentworth: "Personal Identification"

Wall: "Eye-witness Identification in Criminal Cases"

Wiener: "Forensic Importance of Blood Grouping"

Wellman: "The Art of Cross-Examination"

TABLE OF CASES

Table of Cases

Page

Table of Cases